Everyday

Peace

Letters

for

Life

D1015267

Other books by Baba Hari Dass

Yoga Sutras of Patañjali: A Study Guide for Book I

Silence Speaks

The Path to Enlightenment is not a Highway

Ashtanga Yoga Primer

A Child's Garden of Yoga

Fire Without Fuel

Mystic Monkey

Sweeper to Saint

Vinaya Chalisa

The Yellow Book (out of print)

Hairakhan Baba: Known, Unknown (out of print)

EVERYDAY
PEACE
Letters for Life

BABA HARI DASS

SRI RAMA PUBLISHING
Santa Cruz, California

© 2000 Sri Rama Publishing

Editors
Rashmi Sharan
Sarada Diffenbaugh
Dharma Dass Budding

Additional Editing
Atma Timan
Lila Ansell
Pratibha Sharan

Design and Production
Suneel Byers
Kranti Mailliard
Rashmi Sharan
Nancy Miller
Dharani Dass McElheron
Dharma Dass Budding

Sri Rama Publishing
P.O. Box 2550
Santa Cruz, CA 95063

(831) 426-5098 phone
(831) 426-5096 fax
srirampub@aol.com

ISBN 0-918100-21-6
Library of Congress Card Number: 00-110593
First Edition

Printed and bound in the United States of America on Recycled Paper

Dedicated to

Ma Renu

A wise and

compassionate

person

TABLE OF

CONTENTS

INTRODUCTION

Over the years, thousands of people seeking peace have turned to Baba Hari Dass for guidance. Because of his vow of silence, that guidance often comes in the form of personal letters. This book is a collection of those letters.

Peace is our very nature, yet the experience of peace in everyday life is elusive. Why is peace so difficult to maintain? The reason is the ego. Without the ego, there can be no life. Yet this same ego is the source of desires, selfishness, and attachment, all of which separate us from our essential, peaceful nature. What can we do about this paradox?

Babaji tells us that the answer lies in limits, acceptance, and compromise. By limiting the reach of the ego, the mind is calmed. By accepting the cycles of life, the mind is calmed. By living with the spirit of compromise, the mind is calmed. And, it is only when the mind is calm that peace is experienced.

Calming the mind is at the heart of spiritual practice. Obstacles to practice arise, and navigating the spiritual path alone can require the precision of a surgeon, the endurance of a triathlete, and the courage of a hero. For the rest of us, it helps to have direction along the way.

Babaji has been a yogi all his life. He left home at the age of eight to attend a school for young renunciates in the jungles of the lower Himalayas. He was classically trained in traditional Ashtanga Yoga. This eight-limbed yoga includes guidelines for a virtuous life, spiritual practices for calming the mind, and the yogic postures associated with Ashtanga Yoga in the West. He has written commentaries on the traditional yoga scriptures, such as the *Yoga Sutras of Patañjali*, the *Samkhya Karika*, and the *Bhagavad Gita*.

Babaji has maintained continual silence since 1952. He leads the highly disciplined and austere life of a renunciate monk. But instead of encouraging people to live as he does, he guides us to live our own lives. The *Bhagavad Gita* says that it is better for us to do our own duty imperfectly than to do another's duty perfectly. Babaji's teachings echo this wisdom.

Everyday Peace: Letters for Life contains 130 actual responses to questions about how to bring peace to life. Over the past 25 years scores of people have given us copies of their letters from Babaji in anticipation of this book. The letters written to Babaji have not been included, and the writers' names have been removed.

The questions relate to universal life situations, and you will be able to infer them from your own experience. But, the original reader did have a context that we do not have, and there may be an occasional gap in the transition between topics. We believe this is minor compared to the benefit of preserving the letters in their original form.

Babaji's wise responses are useful to all seekers. His letters give simple, direct answers that promote the experience of everyday peace. In fact, it is remarkable how much the letters are about the issues and not about the personalities. At the same time, the letters are warm and personal. The love and care Babaji has for all beings clearly shines.

In *The Spiritual Path*, the first chapter of the book, Babaji advises us to take responsibility for ourselves and our spiritual development. We should be honest to ourselves about our attitudes in life and about the realities of life. When we see clearly how we affect our own experience, we can remove our negativities. Then, love shines naturally in all directions just as light shines out from a lit candle.

Two main themes are present in *Relationships*. The first is that pure love for God and attached love for people are different. Loving God means not hating anyone, including ourselves. God is eternal, so love for God is not bound by the limitations of space and time. On the other hand, love in the world is mixed with ego and attachment, and this is the cause of all relationship problems. The solution to these problems, which is the second main theme of the chapter, is to be in relationship with a spirit of compromise. No one is always right and no one is always wrong. The willingness to compromise is the gateway to peace.

The essence of *God & Religion* is that God is beyond name and form, and cannot be owned by any religion.

The original truth of religion is a direct experience of
God. But over time, the understanding of that truth gets
confused with the rules and rituals of the religion. The
experience of God is available to each of us, regardless of
religious belief. Because the mind cannot worship the
nameless and formless God, it creates names and forms
for God that can be worshiped. This is a very useful
creation, whose purpose is to help us purify the mind,
realize the truth, and merge into the formless.

The chapter *What is Guru?* addresses the many questions about what the right relationship between spiritual
teacher and disciple is. Babaji's constant message is that
peace is most important; a spiritual teacher is one who
helps the studeent realize peace. In order for a spiritual
teacher to be effective, the student must have faith in
the teacher. The work is always on the part of the student,
but the experienced teacher is an invaluable aid along
the way.

Though a master yogi himself, Babaji doesn't put any
requirements on his students to practice one set of methods over another. But, when someone desires to practice
yoga, he tells them the best methods for their nature. In
Yoga Practice & Philosophy, the main theme is that regular
sadhana (spiritual practice) purifies the mind, which
brings peace. Why does sadhana work? Babaji answers
that it is the best way to limit the ego, enabling us to
experience the truth. When we understand the truth for
ourselves, the mind becomes established in real peace,
and all the questions and anxieties of life fall away.

Finally, in *Life & Death*, the main theme that flows through Babaji's letters is that our attitude and approach to life determine our experience of life. There is so much that we cannot change about the world. If we have a negative attitude, all these things appear to be burdensome and full of misery. If we accept life as it is and develop a positive attitude, then life becomes "as light as a feather on an elephant's back." The cycle of life is birth, growth, decay, and death. Nothing in the world is outside this cycle. We have to accept it all if we are to find peace, but most people accept only birth and growth and reject decay and death. Death is a problem for those who do not accept it.

We, the editors of this precious book, are grateful to have worked with it. It has been a joy and an honor, and it has helped each of us on our own spiritual path. Our greatest hope is that you will also find meaning and inspiration from its pages.

In peace,
Rashmi, Sarada, and Dharma Dass
October, 2000

A NOTE ON THE TEXT

This book has been divided into six chapters according to the main themes of the letters. Within the chapters, the letters are also grouped according to topic, and are not arranged in any temporal sequence.

All names have been removed from the letters and replaced with a random first initial followed by a dash, e.g. M—. These initials have no correlation to the original names nor to each other. The M— of one letter is not related to the M— of another.

There is a glossary at the end of the book containing all the Sanskrit terms used in the book. For your convenience, the first use of the Sanskrit in the text has been italicized. All other uses have been left in the roman.

Babaji ends his letters with the symbol representing *Om*. It signifies the infinite, which is omniscient, omnipresent, and omnipotent.

You may notice several recurring themes in Babaji's letters. These are often the most essential truths, yet the ones we need to hear repeatedly before they are accepted.

Finally, the letters have been edited as little as possible. Babaji did not learn English until he was an adult, and we hope the charm of his writing has been maintained.

CHAPTER
ONE

The Spiritual Path

Dear M—,

Contentment, compassion, and tolerance are the three pillars of spirituality. God can't be seen in a form sitting in heaven but can be experienced in loving every person.

You have everything and you want more. It's natural in human beings. You don't need to give away your house, money, and car, and leave your family to find God. The only thing necessary is to understand attachment. What makes us so attached to objects when we know that nothing remains the same and nothing will ever remain the same? You see how a baby sitter takes care of a baby like a mother and doesn't get attached to the baby, yet she does her job perfectly. In the same way you can take care of your family, friends, and property with the non-attachment and care of a baby sitter.

Life is not a burden; we make it a burden. If we accept the law of nature, which is birth, growth, decay, and death, then life will flow in its natural course. We don't accept life as it is. That's why it becomes a burden.

If we feel that we take birth to serve God by serving the creation, then it is also a natural flow. We have so many limitations. We can't change the future and yet we worry about the future. We can't change the past and yet we lament over the past. We can only do one thing, and that is to keep our mind positive in the present.

Dear D—,

Everyone makes mistakes in life. That's the way people learn. No person is 100% perfect. Only God is perfect.

Worldly desires exist until a person attains *samadhi*. The reality of the world can be experienced by the senses. As long as God is not experienced as real as the world is, the mind will only accept this world and will always doubt God.

If one says, "I am a sinner, I am not worthy of attaining liberation," then one can't progress. Liberation is for sinners. Liberation is not for those who are already liberated. So counting your sins and doing nothing will not do any good. Don't dwell in the past and don't worry about the future. Just make your present positive and peaceful.

Dear A—,

Living in a moment and just loving is the hardest thing to do. Normally when we say *the present* we do not mean that moment that joins the past and future. Our present is mixed with the past and the future. For example, if someone says, "I am eating," it is not exactly the present because some food was already eaten and some food has yet to be eaten. But the person includes the past and future with that eating process in the present.

Living in the moment is that awareness of the present that is changing to the past in a moment. If a person is aware of that moment and keeps the mind positive (love), that's the highest stage. Being in high meditation brings the present in a positive state because we are not paying attention to the past and future.

Dear S—,

It is useless to think *Who was I?* and *Who will I be?*
The most important thing is *Who am I?* If we dwell on
our past, which we can't change, or if we dwell on the
future, which is indefinite and unknown, then we can't
work in the present.

If the present is passing in peace, it will make a peaceful past and sow a seed of peace to grow in the future.
Selfless service, desireless love, nonattachment, and
compassion promote peace. All these acts are done in the
present. The present is the most important thing in life,
but we forget the present and either dwell in the past or
worry about the future.

Wish you all happy.

Dear B—,

The aim of life is to live in peace. We are attached to the world through our senses. An individual in the world is continuously giving and taking. Our mind is so busy in this process of giving and taking that we have no time to think *Who am I?* So we don't understand ourselves and remain in ignorance, which is attachment, ego, anger, hate, jealousy, and fear.

The world is not a burden. We make it a burden by our fears, responsibilities, duties, etc. We don't understand the mechanism of nature and we don't include ourselves as a part of that mechanism. We get pain, pleasure, sadness, and happiness because in our mind there is separateness: my house, my wife, my religion, my country, etc. When this *my* and *mine* drop out then there is only one reality, which is God, love, peace.

Wish you happy.

Dear F—,

It never works. You can't find happiness in outer objects because everything is changing, mortal, and unreal. Look inside and go on piercing the darkness. There you will find light.

A mirage gives hope to a thirsty traveler, and that gives the courage to walk faster and find water. But in spite of the hope and courage the traveler still dies because the mirage is not real water. Outer objects are no better than the mirage. Our desires manifest all those objects. If the desire is removed, the objects are like scattered beads of a rosary with a broken string.

Understand your desire to live and your fear of death. As soon as you understand, there is no longer life or death. You will be in perfect peace, a peace that will never wear out, that will never get dim or eliminated. It's a flame of peace unaffected by the wind of desires.

To attain that peace you walk through a very narrow lane of nonattachment. In that lane only one can walk. If there are two, the lane will get clogged and one can't progress. It's a lane for a lonely seeker of light and love. Alone is constant and inexhaustible. Call it peace, truth, or God; it doesn't matter.

Dear R—,

Life is not a burden. We make it a burden by not accepting life as it is. We desire everything. If we don't get what we desire, we feel anger, depression, and pain. If we do get it, then we get attached, jealous, and discontented, which again causes pain. So the root cause is desire (needs, expectations, wants, etc.). If we put a limit on our desires, there will be a limit to our pain. Gradually we can reduce the limit, and one day the desires will be decreased so much that we will not even think about them. That state of mind is peace.

I am happy to know that you are doing your sadhana regularly.

Om shanti, shanti, shanti

Dear W—,

It's good that you are working as a team. About going to India and finding a teacher, if you have a keen desire to go to India, you should go. In India you can learn many things. You can see many things, and you can experience many things.

On one hand you say you want to go India and on the other hand you say, "I don't want to make decisions. If the spirit directs me to go to India, I will go." You see the desire manifesting. You are already desiring to go to India and spirit has nothing to do with it. Probably you will feel that the desire is spirit, which it is not.

Yes, desire is a very subtle thing. It tricks a person by taking many forms. Even in the high stages of trance (samadhi), desires come and appear as if they are God's will. What is desire and what is spirit or God's will can only be determined by purifying the mind.

Wish you all happy.

Dear G—,

The purpose of human birth is to experience the world and to attain liberation. In the world we have several duties: taking good care of the body, responsibility for the family, social duties, etc. All those duties are for experiencing the world. At the same time, our duty is to attain liberation. Liberation is attained by devotion to God, by surrendering to God, and by serving God's creation without any selfish motive.

Yes, a human life is for devotion to God. If one commits his or her life totally to devotion to God, that's the best thing to do. But there is a great pull of the world, which always creates desires, attachment, and possessiveness in the mind and pollutes the devotion. So first we have to limit our desires. Then, the narrower the limit of desires becomes, the more love for God increases.

Dear V—,

   Lust, wealth, and fame are the three desires that pull
the mind of a *yogi* away from sadhana. No one thinks that
time is passing; everyone thinks time is coming. So we
wait and wait for the time to come, and we remain waiting
until one day we see the label of *Old* hanging around our
neck. The mind says, "What did I do for my whole life?"
It sees nothing. The person has attained nothing, gets
frightened, and tries to stick to people. They push that
person away. One gets sad, lonely, and resentful. So
shouldn't we make ourselves independent by developing
our understanding through regular sadhana?

Dear K—,

A human being is born with two desires: one desire is to enjoy the world, experience everything of the world, and go through all pains and pleasures. The other desire is to find God, peace, or truth. The mind alternates between these two desires. They are obstructions to each other, so the mind gets confused. Sometimes the mind is pulled by the world and sometimes the mind is pulled by the feeling of God. The world is a visual reality that is identified by the mind, whereas God is unseen, unexperienced, and doubtful. So the mind likes it better being in the world. But God is a reality that has been known to human beings from the day the first person incarnated on earth.

We are in the world, so we can't just ignore the world. We each have our own social responsibilities. We have our parents, friends, society, country, everything. We have to adjust ourselves to everything and yet we have to find God. So we use a method. The method is to cultivate good qualities like love, compassion, contentment, and honesty. This method purifies the mind and develops a higher consciousness. In that higher consciousness, God's beauty shines by itself.

It is good that you want to work with blind people. It's a selfless service. It also purifies the mind.

Wish you happy.

Dear H—,

The world always pulls us to attachment, desires, lust, greed, etc. This is a natural flow of the mind in the world. It's like a river that naturally flows down the slope of the land. But the aim of life is to get back to the source. So it means we have to climb up. Climbing up requires two things: first you have be detached from the place where you are, which is the world, and second you have to apply continuous effort. If you stop trying you can't progress and it is more likely that you may slip down. In simple words we say that by dispassion for the world and persistent practice of spiritual methods, one can reach to the source, which is God.

Dear U—,

In the world there is no peace, happiness, or contentment. There are desires, needs, and expectations. But we can use the world as a tool to get out of the world, just like a thorn is used to pull out a thorn from your foot.

We can't avoid this outer reality. We have to be in society; we have to work to earn a livelihood. We have to face our emotions. But if our aim is strong, then all our activities will become supportive of our aim. For example, a thief goes to break into a house at night. If he sees a rope, a pole, a tree, a ladder, a nail, all these things become supports for his actions. Exactly the same thing happens if your aim is to find God. You meet bad people and your mind sees the result of bad actions. You see anger, hate, and jealousy, and your mind learns how it harms you. In this way the world teaches us how to get out of the world.

The main thing is selfless service. It sounds easy but it is very hard. Our mind is so selfish that whatever we do, the mind always seeks its own benefit. But in the beginning we work simply with the thought of serving others. Gradually the subtlety of selfishness begins to show and we remove selfish desires.

Dear R—,

Failure is the foundation of success. We learn how to achieve success by failing in our efforts. The main thing is to not stop the effort.

In the spiritual path what are our expectations? What do we mean by *I failed?* Probably we want to be on the top of Mount Everest with very little experience in climbing. But if we go on climbing, we can achieve success.

The main thing in the spiritual path is developing positive qualities. Every second of our lives should be positive and that is devotion. We can pray, chant, worship a picture, deity, or a symbol of God, but if the mind is not developing positive qualities, then our progress will stop.

Dear B—,

Ego always gets in the way, but if you understand your ego, then it can't possess your mind. There is always some ego in everything. One should beware of the ego turning to the negative side. Positive ego is important for progress in the world as well as in the spiritual path. Complete elimination of ego is liberation.

Do your work by surrendering to God. Don't think that you are helping others, but think that God is helping them, taking you as an instrument.

Dear P—,

It's good that you are feeling God's presence in your heart. People get afraid when the mind starts dwelling on God because they feel they will not be able to enjoy the pleasures of the world if they are merged into God. For them the world is real. It is because the world can be identified with our senses, whereas God is beyond our senses. But the aim of life is to find God, whether we do it in this life or in future lives.

Dear J—,

The purpose of life is to experience the world and get liberation from all experiences. You are questioning why you are here and what is the purpose of your life. Life is for living and then leaving. As long as you live in this reality, accept it. Sometimes you may feel sad, but it's all part of life. Just like the change of weather creates sickness in people like cough, colds, and flu, while all the time it's nature's method of purifying the body. In the same way, happiness, sadness, pain, and pleasure simply purify the mind by developing an understanding of why all this happens.

Dear M—,

The mind always goes through different stages, sometimes negative and sometimes positive. When the mind dwells in the negative, we have to discover the cause. There is always some self-interest that creates negativity. Discontentment begins when we don't get what we want. If this want is identified as selfishness, then everything changes.

Human birth is the highest. It is for attaining liberation. If we don't consciously try for liberation, then we are misusing our human birth. Every action, thought, and word should be spiritual. It happens only when the mind is purified by sadhana.

Dear C—,

Jai Sita Ram.

Self is God. Still there is a difference between our will and God's will as long as we don't find God within ourselves. For finding God within ourselves we need complete surrender to God. Complete surrender doesn't mean not to work, not to eat, or not to meet people, but it refers to the ego. The notion *I am the doer* should be eliminated from the mind.

What happens then? The mind begins to accept all situations and becomes free from pleasure and pain. It develops dispassion, and dispassion brings enlightenment.

In words the method seems very easy. But it's very difficult to surrender. It needs practice in every action. Without watching ourselves we can't be aware of the tricks our mind plays. So a yogi should be alert and watchful within, all the time.

My love and Jai Sita Ram to your husband, parents, and to all spiritual people.

Dear N—,

We can support all our evil deeds and actions by saying, "It's my *samskaras*." In this way a killer, a thief, and a rapist can justify their wrong acts. But samskaras are the seeds of good and bad actions. These seeds can grow only by creating the right conditions. The conditions are created by the mind. We have a mind that can think, decide, discriminate, and realize the effects of our actions. So the mind gives the right soil for all our actions to grow. The mind is responsible for right and wrong acts.

Dear S—,

A monk meditates in a cave for himself. A candle that is not lit cannot give light. A monk who meditates in a cave is in the process of lighting his candle. When the candle is lit, its light will spread by itself, and all those who are not blind can use that light.

There are people in the world who are not aware of right and wrong, who don't know their aim, who pass their time in taking drugs, gambling, and cheating. What benefit to the world is their existence? But if those same people come close to a candle's light (light of the saint), their lives can change.

A monk tries to attain the truth in himself and when it is attained, that truth shines and the world benefits from his light. Sometimes living in a cave is running away from the responsibilities of the world. It happens when a person doesn't know his real aim.

The real cave is your own heart. The main idea is to search inside, but it's not so easy because the mind is distracted by objects. So a monk chooses a place where there are less distractions from objects. When the mind is trained to remain detached among objects, then no cave, no seclusion is needed. The whole world becomes a cave.

Dear T—,

Satsang means union with the truth. The truth can only be revealed when people meet each other without any ego, the ego of name, fame, wealth, etc.

There is a story about *Krishna*. Once while all the *gopis* (Krishna's cowherd girl devotees) were taking a bath in the Yamuna river without any clothes on, Krishna secretly came and took away their clothes and climbed a tall tree. When the gopis finished their bath, they saw their clothes hanging on the tree. They did not come out of the water and prayed to Krishna to return their clothes. Their body consciousness prevented them from coming out of the water. This story has deep meaning. Krishna is God (transcendental consciousness). The gopis are *jiva* (individual consciousness). The water is *maya* (illusion). As long as a jiva has body consciousness, they can't come out of the illusion even though they see God near them.

In the same way the ego consciousness stops us from seeing the truth. When the clothes of these egos are thrown away, then all become one.

My love and Jai Sita Ram to everyone.

Dear I—,

Simple and straight-forward understanding is better than complicated philosophies. I make it very simple for myself, which is *Keep God's presence in my heart and move on*. I don't think about life after death or about what I should do for others. If my heart and mind are in a positive place then all actions of the mind and functions of the body are being guided by that divine power. So why should *I* think about helping, serving, or doing things? *I* should just go on and everything will happen by itself.

The future is unknown. Whenever we walk toward the unknown, we carry a lamp. In worldly-minded people, that lamp is the ego, and in spiritually-minded people, the lamp is divine presence. Both are walking toward the same unknown, dark space; one is afraid and the other is fearless.

Everyone will die; that is as real as the sun will set. But human beings live in a state forgetful of death. This forgetfulness of death brings attachment to life. That attachment creates the individual's world.

Keep the lamp lit, walk on step by step. You can't go astray, but will merge in the light.

Dear V—,

When the sun rises, night no longer remains. A person who has realized God can't be in worldly pain, because for that person there is no world in existence.

When you put sugar into your tea the sugar loses its separate form. You don't think *it's sugar and tea*, you just think *it's tea*. People who have realized God become God even though they still possesses human qualities. They eat like others, talk, play, and feel sorry, and have pain and pleasure. But it's only the gross body's functions. Their subtle body does not acquire any samskaras from their actions.

A man who has a ten dollar bill in his pocket but does not know it is there possesses ten dollars but also doesn't possess ten dollars. Because he isn't aware of it he might even ask others to give him ten dollars. But as soon as he realizes that the ten dollars is in his pocket, he stops asking for money.

In the same way, God is within us but we don't possess God as long as we are not aware of God. As soon as we are aware of God, we don't ask others about God. The man who becomes aware of ten dollars in his own pocket becomes so happy that he starts dancing, singing, and telling others about the money. The same thing happens to a person who becomes aware of God within himself.

Attachment to God is devotion. Attachment is painful in this world and also in the spiritual world. But the pain of the world is from ignorance and illusion, while the pain of the spiritual world is from love and wisdom.

It's not necessary for everybody to get flashes of light, rumbling of clouds, or disappearing sun in the sky. As there is much difference in the nature, in the physical bodies, and in the samskaras of people, feelings are also different in each person. The main thing is depth of concentration, faith in God and in your own sadhana, and attachment to God.

Wish you all happy and success in sadhana.

Dear D—,

Love is a light that shines by itself. It cannot be given or borrowed. It can't be shown if it is not already within us.

Love develops when the mind is purified. Impure mind is nothing but our anger, hate, jealousy, egoism, vanity, and pride. Its cause is selfish desires. The more we reduce our selfish desires the more our mind gets purified, and the more the light of love shines and is felt by others.

The love that we feel in the social level is actually attachment. In that attachment there is self-interest. In the love for a child, for parents, or for friends, there is some self-interest and attachment but there is also pure love that creates a tight bond.

Another love is self-surrender. When we don't keep the ego of being a doer, we surrender our ego to that supreme power, which is explained as supreme consciousness, supreme existence, and supreme bliss, the absolute Lord of the universe. Then all the coverings of ignorance drop away from our heart and there remains only pure love, a universal love in which no differentiation, no judgement, and no discrimination exist.

CHAPTER
TWO

Relationships

Dear L—,

What is love? It is a question that is only answered by experience. Words are never enough to explain it, but we can still try. Love is a state of mind free from all selfish desires. But on the worldly level, can we live without selfish desires? We need to love and to be loved. On the worldly level, the term *love* means attachment to a person based on equality, intimacy, and sharing. There is trust, mutual support, and complete acceptance. However, the nature of the human mind is change, so love that starts with attachment, acceptance, trust, and mutual support, wears out. Then the mind starts looking for something new. The wheel of love based on attachment starts out bringing pleasure, but then moves in different directions bringing pain, misery, discontentment, and anger.

Love for God is very different because it is not based on attachment. There can still be intense pain and sadness from the feeling of separation. But by understanding our aim in life, we can change that feeling of separation from God to devotion.

To love someone in the world, we need either the physical presence of that person or a memory of them. To love the formless, eternal, and infinite God, we create a form. That created form for God is called *ishta deva*, or god of your desire adored by you. Different people in India have their ishta devas such as Rama, Vishnu, Shiva, Krishna, Hanuman, Kali, and Durga. In other religions they also have ishta devas.

If you have not found a partner on the worldly level you are still with your inner partner, the Self or God, which can never be separated from you.

It will be good if you attend Yoga Teacher Training. Wishing you success in your sadhana.

Dear A—,

There is nothing greater than loving God. To love God we have to love God's creation. To feel God's love we should accept ourselves first, because we are also within God's creation. If you feel self-rejection, self-hatred, or self-pity, you are not loving God's creation.

You say you are lonely and can't feel love from others. It's simply a self-created idea that no one loves you. I will give you an example of a self-created idea: A woman marries a man and establishes the relationship of wife and husband. She feels like a wife. But when she divorces the man, she wipes out that idea and doesn't feel like the wife of that man. It's simply an acceptance and rejection in the mind. The marriage itself doesn't cause any relationship to occur. The marriage document doesn't create the relationship. It's only the mind that forms an idea.

If you form an idea that people love you and you are not alone, your mind will wipe out the idea of being unloved and lonely.

You say you don't have a lover or boyfriend. You can have a boyfriend if you make yourself happy, loving, and positive. How would you feel if you were with a man who is depressed, angry, or overly emotional? Your mind would not like it. In the same way a man expects a girlfriend to be happy, cheerful, playful, and loving.

Probably you are afraid to love a man. You love your cat because you are not afraid that the cat will demand love. If you want to share love with a man, first accept yourself. Don't think of yourself as miserable, lonely, and full of pain.

Dear T—,

One can be open, loving, and sharing with all and still maintain the worldly relationships, i.e., brother, sister, mother, father, husband, friends. To be one with everybody doesn't mean that a man should treat his mother and wife the same and have sex with both. They are the same in their own essential nature but differ according to their relationship.

When we say *same*, we mean not to hate one person and love another person. *Same* doesn't mean you have to see their forms as the same or their relationship as the same. On the physical level they are different.

For example, take a man and woman. Both are the *same*, but their functions are different. You can't expect a man to give birth to a child because that is not his function.

You love your husband and you have a particular bond with him. You love your brother and you have a different kind of bond with him. In this way you relate to each person differently, but there is a sameness, which is that you don't hate anyone.

You are confusing yourself by mixing sex with love. Love is a feeling untouched by desires. This love should be the same for everyone.

Every person in the world is different. You can't find two people with exactly the same fingerprints. There are physical differences and differences in relationships. You can't share everything with everybody. This is not possible. You may share something with your husband, but not with your brother or father.

May God bring you peace.

Dear S—,

I received your letter dated the 20th. I was away until last night, so today is the first chance I have to answer it.

There is no end to desires. Everything looks beautiful, magical, and attractive when we desire it. When we don't desire that thing, it appears in its real form. Go on chasing one woman after another. There will be no satisfaction. Satisfaction comes only from limiting desires. That's why wise people made a rule of marriage and one-to-one relationships.

How strange it is that you have a beautiful, loving, intelligent, healthy wife and still your mind goes to another. It is said that kings in the past always enjoyed sex with their ugly maidservants and avoided their beautiful queens. It's only desire that wipes out the ability to discriminate and so a person starts jumping from one thing to another. For a peaceful life surrender to each other and be faithful to each other.

Dear C—,

Jai Sita Ram.

It's good that you are visiting your parents and trying to make them happy. But you feel that your father does not accept spirituality. I think your judgment about your father is not correct. He accepts spirituality according to his own ideas and understanding, whereas in your mind you have made a set form of spirituality.

Spirituality doesn't mean not to work or take responsibility in the world. Spirituality doesn't mean to have long hair, beard, and mustache. Spirituality doesn't mean to wear rags and walk without shoes and to not observe bodily cleanliness. Spirituality doesn't mean to take drugs and get high on daydreams.

Spirituality is a personal thing. It is purity of heart, mind, and actions. To be spiritual one doesn't need to wear any labels, a certain dress, have a special name, or join a certain religion.

There is a time gap between parents and children. This time gap can't be filled because time is always changing. In twenty years everything becomes different. But parents do not want to accept the change in their children. They want them to be exactly as they were. Those parents who accept this change in time can relate to their children comfortably. For those who don't, a wall remains between them. Your father will accept you if he sees any practical, positive change in you. So make yourself better all the time in your personal, social, and spiritual life.

Dear H—,

Romance, marriage, pregnancy, childbirth: in these four stages a husband and wife don't really know what is happening. After childbirth a mother gets attached to the child and feels responsible for the family. In her mind the child becomes her life and her world. Then the husband feels neglected and gets jealous of the child and yet he also loves the child. He is torn in opposite directions and acts crazy. All husbands go through this stage to a greater or lesser degree after the first child is born. This is the cause of most separations after the birth of the first child.

I think your husband loves you but uses his bitterness toward you to get your attention in order to be accepted by you one hundred percent.

Nowadays people use terms like *sucked in*, *insecure*, and *lighten up* when they want someone to listen to them. Do you know we all are insecure in some ways; we all are *sucked into* our own confusion? That's why we try to make our life happy and peaceful. Night and day can't coexist at the same time. If we are not happy and in peace, then we are insecure.

The break up of a family is not good. You and your husband should talk about your problems honestly. No one in the world is one hundred percent perfect. You can't be right all the time and you aren't wrong all the time. Because there is a disagreement creeping in, you both see the other as wrong.

People can use yoga, *ashrams*, and communities as hideouts. It's true, but those who are not into yoga and ashrams also can make different kinds of hideouts, like drugs, not meeting people, etc. Anything can be used as a hideout if a person has no definite aim.

You should try hard to make your marriage successful. May God help you both.

Dear N—,

Love never makes conditions. It's like a woman saying to a man, "I love you and I'll marry you only if you grow to be six feet tall." The man can wear high-heel shoes to be six feet tall but it's not reality. In the same way, you can't pretend to be happy, loving, and enjoying yourself. You are guided by your samskaras. Your samskaras can change only by sadhana.

No one in the world is perfectly happy. People are attached to their sense of pleasure and when it doesn't manifest perfectly, they get pain.

In an honest relationship two people accept each other's bright side as well as their dark side. If they accept only the bright side and expect only love, happiness, and joy in life and reject pain, sadness, and sorrow, then the relationship can't exist for long. A relationship is a surrender. In surrendering you don't choose.

Yes, the mind is the creator of everything. You create heaven and you create hell. Both are in the mind. Yoga sadhana deals with the mind. If the mind is controlled, then everything else is easy to control. As long as the mind is busy in talking to itself, it never listens to the Self. So first we have to silence the mind and then we can hear the song of God within the Self.

Wish you happy and in love with God.

Dear D—,

We all make mistakes. We all have negative tendencies. No one is perfect. So I cannot say that it is all your fault. J— should not be violent to show you the truth. There is no violence in truth. Violence comes when a desire is obstructed or encroached upon. When there is desire, then it is not the whole truth. So everyone who seeks the truth should be peaceful, tolerant, and compassionate.

When two people live together, they sometimes disagree with each other but it doesn't mean that they should fight and become violent.

To find fault with others becomes a habit. But if we are capable of finding our own faults in everyday activities, we can really progress. In fact, what we see in others are our own weaknesses and faults. Everyone becomes everyone else's mirror but we don't want to accept our own faults, so we do not use these mirrors to improve ourselves.

If any disagreement arises, you both can talk about it peacefully. If it remains unsettled, then you can ask some third party to give their advice or opinion. You have a child now and you both are responsible for your child, so you should bring your marriage together because the child completes the triangle: Father – Mother – Child.

Wish you all happy and in peace.

Dear V—,

Jai Sita Ram.

It's a wrong notion that someone can bring happiness into your life. There are so many couples who are very unhappy but I understand the need for a mate. It's a natural desire. You want a man who will love you, but that love should be received by love. Otherwise you will still feel unhappy.

So, the first thing is to develop contentment, tolerance, and compassion within yourself. Everyone is attracted to peace. No one likes anger, hate, and jealousy. If you develop peace inside, all men will be attracted to you.

It's not right to think that no one loves you. It makes you depressed, sad, and unhappy. If you develop positivity in your mind, you will find that you are surrounded by positive people.

Wishing you happy and healthy.

Dear B—,

I received your letter. I am sorry to hear that you are unhappy. If you and your husband love each other, there is no reason to file for divorce. In your husband's letter he wrote that you left him and do not want to take responsibility for your son.

I understand that such problems come to all couples. The main reason is expectations. It is like a horse who is grazing in a grassy field and thinks there will be better grass ahead so he starts looking for better grass. After all, both you and your husband are human beings. You both have your desires, expectations, and weaknesses. Just one person can't take the blame for your separation and just one won't get the whole credit for your reunion.

When people separate, they find similar partners again because partners of similar samskaras get together to work out their problems. So they go through the same problems again and they begin to see their mistakes in their previous relationships. But time passes and never returns. Before filing for divorce you both should realize that you will not get anything new by it. The same problems will repeat, so why don't you solve the problems right now without breaking up your marriage?

Compassion and tolerance are the foundation of marriage. May God bless you both.

Dear P—,

Jai Sita Ram.

Your children make a world of your family. God and the creation are not separate. To love God we have to love God's creation, which is visible and can be identified. Your family is a miniature form of this vast creation. If you serve your children, you are serving the whole creation.

Longing for God is the first step of spirituality. It is strengthened by devotion, compassion, friendliness, and love for all beings.

Renunciation is a mental attitude. Renounce the attachment to the objects but not the object itself. Celibacy is a good thing but in married life it can only be observed when both parties agree to it. Otherwise it will cause separation. The separation of couples is very bad for children.

The best way for a householder to live a spiritual life is to serve their family with a feeling that God is in them. Contentment, compassion, and tolerance are to be practiced in all acts of life. In this way life will get purer everyday and peace will be attained.

Dear R—,

Jai Sita Ram.

I received your letter, You asked many questions about your relationship with L—.

1. Strengthen your love for each other by being honest with each other.

2. You don't have to marry right away but you should both keep in mind that by being together you are heading toward marriage.

3. If there is love between you, then age difference does not matter.

4. You say, "What can I give to him in a marriage?" In a marriage both giver and taker become one. They do not even think about who is giving what. This is hard to do but everyone should try.

5. Marriage is yoga, a unity of two people who agree to carry the burden of life together peacefully.

6. Ups and downs always come in a marriage, while living with one person, in a group, community, or tribe. This is because the mind changes all the time. We have emotions, differences in opinions and ideas, and we have our own good and bad samskaras. These cause changes in us from time to time that result in anger, pain, happiness, depression, and joy. But we can learn to adjust to all these situations. That adjustment is called *tapas*.

7. It's not right to marry someone thinking of divorce. Slowly develop your love and understand each other. May God bring you happiness.

ॐ

Dear A—,

No one can have everything. We gain something and we lose something. In this way life goes on.

Tolerance, compassion, and contentment: without developing these three qualities we can't live together and can't love each other. A married couple should sacrifice their personal desires and row their boat together.

What you say about negativity is not unusual. It exists in every person. But we have to overcome these things by watching ourselves. You have made a family. In a family we are free to do some things individually and we have to do some things collectively.

There is no peace if there is no limitation of desires. That's why we make rules—to imprison our desires.

You have known your husband for a long time. If you love each other, you have to tolerate each other's faults.

It's a very hard austerity to live with a person. It requires much sacrifice. If you think you will find a better person, there is no limit to better. You will go on searching and you will not find any man who is one hundred percent perfect. So your whole life will pass away in pain and when old age comes, you will feel very alone.

In a few cases it becomes impossible to live together. For example, a person goes crazy or develops a bad habit, like drug addiction or gambling. But this occurs in only five percent of the cases. In ninety-five percent of the cases, if people marry out of real love, they can adjust their lives. When old age comes, they are a support for each other because in Western culture the young society rejects them.

Dear C—,

Jai Sita Ram.

Women get afraid when they are 30. Up to the age of 29 they consider themselves young and when they hit 30 they categorize themselves differently. Again ages 45 and 50 are depressing for them. Men get depressed at the ages of 40 and 60.

The desire for sex is in the mind. At those ages a woman thinks that her time for physical enjoyment is running away. If she wants to enjoy sex or have children, then she feels she has to do it fast. It leads her to more sex. Also, fear develops, and people start worrying more for the future. They start clinging to the idea of material success. While some cling to the idea of spiritual success, most people don't think much about spiritual success because the desire for material success gets very strong.

You say you can't do meditation, *asanas*, or *pranayamas*. These are methods to get control over the mind. One can develop control by understanding the aim, by understanding oneself, and by understanding the energy that is blocking one from progressing. Between God and the self, the blocking energy is our ego. If the ego is pulled toward the world it becomes a wall. If the same ego is pulled toward God it becomes a ladder.

In *Nada Yoga*, breath retention is not very important. The most important thing is nada (sound). There is no visualization. You have to concentrate on the *bija* sound, which is always a variation of Om.

Just sit comfortably and listen to nada. That's all you have to do.

ॐ

Dear V—,

There is no end to desires. There is a momentary satisfaction, but this too leads to discontentment. The marriage system is based on a one-to-one relationship, and it creates a limit to desires. When a person doesn't create any limits in a relationship, then what happens? The person's mind dwells on sensual gratification all the time. But it ends in discontentment, which is the greatest pain of life.

You and S— don't get along in your marriage because there is no surrender in your mind. Your ego tells you that you should seek a better man. To support your desire you have to defend your beliefs, actions, and needs. When there is surrender in a marriage, then there is complete acceptance and the question of defending your beliefs, thoughts, and needs doesn't arise.

Unresolved problems sit on a person's shoulder like a ghost. Anywhere the person goes, the ghost is right there. As long as you think that you can always find another man, you can't adjust to life with S— with honesty, cheerfulness, and peace.

So look within and identify your desires and find out if they will ever be satisfied. If not, then live within the limits of your marriage.

Wishing you happy and healthy.

Dear J—,

Jai Sita Ram.

If anyone asks a question verbally or in a letter, I have
to answer. I know that people who write letters expect an
answer. If we don't reply, the person's expectations are
shattered. Sometimes not replying to a letter is the reply
that the writer expects and so that person doesn't wait
for an answer.

I don't know the history of St. Valentine. It's enough
for me that he was a saint. All saints appear in this world
to spread love, peace, and friendship. People remember
St. Valentine for his love toward others and we should
learn from his teachings about the love that is not polluted
by selfish desires.

Your negative attitude toward men is based on an
inequality between men and women that was created by
men in the past. No one knows when it started. Physically men are stronger. Emotionally women are stronger. It
creates a balance, but people who don't see this balance
feel that one or the other is superior. It's ignorance. Men
and women are the two equal parts of the same seed. One
part of the seed alone is not complete and can't grow. Both
parts must be together. It's the natural process.

Dear T—,

True love is free from self-interest. In true love there is equality. In true love there is sacrifice of personal desires. People here believe in romance and not in true love. Romance is a state of excitement due to the desire for each other.

In my previous letter, I meant that you are well established in California and it will not be easy for you to just leave everything and go to Florida. Moreover, California is a better place for you than Florida.

P— is a good man. The relationship can be good but you have to see how much he will sacrifice for the relationship. If you leave everything in California and go to Florida, it will be your sacrifice and P— gets everything with no sacrifice. In true love there must be sacrifice on both sides. If you travel to Florida for two months, then the next time he can travel to California for two months.

Desire, ego, and attachment are wrong only when they are not identified with their negative effects.

Yes, you have to think twice about your relationship with P—. How much does he want the relationship with you and how much does he want to sacrifice for the relationship? In romance one doesn't see the reality. In reality there is no romance. So you discover the reality when the romance stage passes away. Everything is God's will whether it is good or bad. It becomes human will when human beings apply their individual desires and egos to worldly events.

Wishing you happy and healthy.

Dear G—,

I am sorry to hear that your beloved husband left this world. May God give peace to his departed soul.

Two people came together in the wife and husband relationship by their samskaras (imprints of the past lives). It's a relationship that is preplanned and it remains in the future life. Your husband's physical body is not with you, but he is with you in the form of love, memories, and subtle energies that were exchanged in your union.

You can't see the physical form of your husband. The physical body takes birth, grows, decays, and dies but the real being never dies. It is passed on from one body to another. The time and space that come in between make a veil of illusion and we can't see the same person in a different body.

By pure love, pure mind, and pure action this illusion is removed and then we can see who is who. Your husband is always with you.

Wish you happy.

Dear I—,

About children, we have to know that children copy anything they see. If they are with good people, they become good and if they are with bad people, they become bad. Just like we train our pets in the house, in the same way the children are also disciplined. If we don't train a pet animal, there are always problems. Sometimes we get angry and feel hatred toward the animal. The same thing happens with children. If they are disciplined and well behaved, no problem arises and they turn out very successful in their future life. If they are left undisciplined, they cause problems first in the family and then in society.

When you start something with children, always keep in mind that discipline is the most important thing. Otherwise there can't be stability in that project.

I am happy to learn that you are developing devotion for God. The aim of a human being is to attain peace. Whether we are aware of it or not, it is always there. Those who become aware of this aim are called awakened. They start a conscious effort to attain God and they get success. Those who are not conscious of it go through numerous ups and downs, but finally they also wake up.

Jai Sita Ram to your husband and children.

Dear M—,

There is no separation in real love. If there is only physical attachment, it can't last long because all that is new will get old some day. Real love is evergreen, unchangeable, and unbreakable. It shines by itself and that is God.

I can imagine your pain. Attachment holds people together and attachment makes pain. So life always goes back and forth between pleasure and pain. We get something and we lose something.

Peace is there when desires are limited. Without limitation of desires, a person is like a deer who runs in a desert chasing a mirage of water without ever finding real water.

Sadhana must be regular and then you will see that worldly pleasures and pains come and go, but your mind will remain unaffected.

Wish you happy and in peace.

CHAPTER
THREE

God & Religion

Dear I—,

I am happy to learn that your devotion for God is growing. I'll be with you in your work for God even if I leave physically. So you should not worry about it.

The important thing is to see the world positively. God created it with some purpose. Everything in creation has some purpose. So we have to respect nature—animals, plants, oceans, rivers, mountains, etc. By respecting God's creation we respect God. By loving God's creation, we love God. We can't see God but we can see God in creation. To find God, we don't have to run around. God is everywhere—inside and outside of us. It's only a matter of accepting God in creation with an honest mind.

Contentment, compassion, and love are important in order to develop a positive attitude.

Dear A—,

You asked about enlightenment and religion. Enlightenment means Self-realization. A religion only teaches how to live a spiritual life in the world. But for achieving Self-realization one should go beyond religions. One should break the sense of individuality and achieve universality where no religion exists. There is only universal consciousness.

When a candle is lit, its light spreads out by itself. Anyone who comes in the proximity of the lit candle can see the light and get its benefit. So, the first thing is to light the inner candle (heart), and then its light (love) will spread out by itself. Anyone who comes in the proximity of that heart will get healed.

May God bring success to your sadhana.

Dear C—,

I believe in Jesus, Mohammed, Buddha, Krishna, and Rama—all avatars and high saints. All those who are enlightened are one. God can't be two. All those who merge in God become one.

Fanaticism is not devotion. It's a type of anger that is projected onto others. God is one and paths are many. If we reject other paths, we do not accept God's infiniteness. We are putting a false limit on God by saying, "This is God and this is the only way."

I am glad to hear that your wife and son are healthy.

Dear W—,

The oceans, the mountains, the rivers, the land, and all living beings are the same in the East and the West. The truth doesn't change because of time and space. So the path of truth is the same everywhere. It is up to us whether we see things with a clear mind or with a deluded mind.

People of the same religion kill each other because of simple disagreements in philosophy. People kill each other because they practice different religions. People kill each other because they have a different color, country, or culture. But still they think they worship God. It's very hard for me to accept these things that their religions allow them to do.

The aim of life is to attain God, which is omnipresent, omniscient, and omnipotent. Truth, love, and reality are all terms for that same God. If one is seeking God, it does not matter which path the person follows.

Wishing you happy and healthy.

Dear L—,

God is one with no name and no form; limitless, omnipresent, omniscient, and omnipotent. If we say, "This is God and this is the only path," then we are putting limits on God. We are reducing God's vastness.

People have no scale for measuring the vastness of God. Ramakrishna Paramahamsa said, "A doll made of salt tried to measure the depth of the ocean and melted on the way." For us God's limit is where we are absorbed in God, but in reality God is much more than that.

If you have to eat apples in a garden, you don't need to count apple trees. When you go to church, you have to do your prayers and worship and not look at others, see how they dress, how they sing, and how they act.

There have been great saints in all religions. By not accepting other religions we are not accepting God in total. In fact all these high saints broke out of the limits of their religions and became one.

We talk of universality and yet we fight and divide God with religions. There can't be universal love as long as there is no acceptance of other religions. Even in one religion they don't accept their different branches. You can see it in Dublin and Belfast, and between the black Christian church and the white Christian church, between Shia Moslems and Sunni Moslems, between Hinayana Buddhists and Mahayana Buddhists, and between Vaishnava Hindus and Shaiva Hindus.

Yoga is not a religion. It's a science to attain peace, enlightenment, and liberation. Any person of any faith or religion can practice yoga.

Dear M—,

The mind always seeks for worldly pleasures because these are perceived as reality. God is not visible; there is no direct proof that God is sitting somewhere, giving peace and happiness to people. So people don't have real faith that there is a God. When they are in pain, they think of God as one who will remove their pain. But when they have pleasure, they forget about God. In this way the mind dwells in confusion and nothing is attained.

One who accepts God never gets confused.

Dear D—,

Truth, reality, or God cannot be owned by any religion, church, temple, or mosque. God does not belong to someone just because they read scriptures, wear robes, or live in caves.

No one can give the experience of God to another. It's like explaining about sweetness without tasting it. God is realized by purity of mind. No religion, church, temple, teacher, or priest is needed to realize God. One who is positive in their actions, thoughts, and words can attain God even while sitting in the center of a market.

It's all right if you work as a priest in a church. You can tell the truth, but people like to be tricked. They want a priest to tell them that he will pray for them, that he will remove all their pain by the power of his prayer, and that he will ask God to grant heaven to them. They don't like to hear that they are responsible for their lives, that they have to pray, they have to meditate, and they have to seek God by regular sadhana.

I am happy to read in your letter, "I do not want to cause or create any mischief in the lives of others, mischief that might arise out of my own blindness and ignorance."

We are putting limits on the unlimited God by making a religion around God. We are dividing God, who is one and only one, by making various religions. We are giving a name and a form to God, to that which has no name and form. In this way we are reducing the vastness of God.

Wish you happy and success in your sadhana.

Dear G—,

I accept what you wrote in your letter about religions, deities, belief systems, and judging people by their religions.

God is formless, attributeless, infinite, eternal energy. God neither punishes the sinners nor rewards the virtuous. That infinite conscious energy simply activates the energy of nature, and nature becomes a god with form and attributes. Those who worship nature are indirectly worshipping the infinite, eternal, attributeless, formless conscious principle (God).

Religions start with an enlightened being's experience of truth. That truth is passed on through the instrument of the human mind and gets colored by the mind's own ego and understanding. As that coloring evolves, the religion does not remain an expression of universal truth but becomes a truth only for its followers.

Truth is not owned by any religion. One who doesn't belong to any religion can experience the highest truth through their own purity of mind.

Dear N—,

You asked me about the Gods of different religions. God is one but is worshiped by different religions in different ways. There have been high saints in every religion, and they have all said the same thing.

If someone says, "My religion is the only religion and my way is the only way," it's okay for that person. But we know it's not the truth because saints from all religions have attained enlightenment.

Faith, devotion, and right aim are the keys to attaining God. It's not the religion or the method that brings enlightenment. A priest can memorize all the scriptures and can preach about scriptures but still remain in ignorance. On the other hand, a person who loves God, surrenders to God, and keeps their mind on good qualities like compassion, contentment, honesty, and love doesn't need any method, scripture, or particular religion. God will accept that person and shine through them.

My love and Jai Sita Ram to your family.

Dear D—,

Jai Sita Ram.

All religions teach how to find God, whether it is outside or inside, with a form or formless.

No one can attain God through a religion. It can be attained only by faith, devotion, and positive qualities. You can wear the label of any religion or the robes of a priest or monk but that can't give you heaven. Heaven is not somewhere outside. It is the eternal peace inside, which is attained by samadhi.

You say Christianity promises heaven and Buddhism promises nothing. Christianity promises heaven on conditions, which are faith and devotion. One can't attain heaven merely by accepting the word *Christian*. You have to work hard to develop your faith and devotion.

In Buddhism they don't believe in God. They believe in Nothingness. So how can they promise something when there is nothing?

It seems you are afraid of death and want to hold on to some religion as a support. Religion can't save anyone from death. Even the prophets, avatars, and *siddhas* got sick, suffered pain, and died.

Reality is not owned by any religion. Honesty, truthfulness, compassion, nonviolence, and love can be practiced by any person. One who practices these qualities will surely attain heaven even if the person doesn't accept any particular religion.

Yes, it's true that in all religions women were not given much encouragement and support. But in the Upanishads it is clearly mentioned that women are religiously equal to men. They were given equal rights in performing spiritual practices.

If you want to love Christ because Christianity promises heaven, that's not a proper reason. Love for God should be unconditional. We have to separate God from our miseries in the world. Birth, growth, decay, and death is the cycle of nature. We have to go through this cycle whether we accept a religion or not.

Wish you happy.

Dear J—,

As long as there is a mind, it will be noisy. The mind's nature is to talk. It talks even when no one listens to it. But when the mind is transformed to higher consciousness, it doesn't talk. It simply sees things.

Yoga sadhana trains and disciplines the mind until gradually it stops talking. It takes time. It takes time only because we like our mind to talk. We are afraid of its silence. We don't want to lose contact with the world to which we are connected through the mind.

Any medicine that cures the disease should be taken. If Judaism can stop your mind from talking, then that is the right medicine for you. Rituals are for devotional people. *Jñana Yoga* works for some. For others, meditation, *Hatha Yoga*, etc. God has shown us millions of paths. It's up to us to choose the right one.

There is no law that if I am a Hindu I must be enlightened, or if I am a Christian I must go to heaven, etc. All those ideas are created by the followers of a religion.

All religions are ruled by priests, spiritual leaders, and wealthy people. They are not enlightened. They have the same pains and miseries of ignorance as the average person. But we have to follow those people because they have power.

Yoga is not a religion. Any person of any religion can practice yoga. It's a scientific path for training the mind. People do various things together as a group like *arati*, *tantra*, *kirtan*, and short skits. It's a way of satisfying their minds. These things are unrelated to yoga but give energy to some people.

Dear P—,

It's good that you have developed faith and devotion for God. God is one and is accepted by different religions in their own way.

Yes, there is power in prayer. When we have faith and devotion, our prayers become true. Without faith and devotion, praying is like a parrot chanting a spiritual song.

When a saint loses egoism (a separate identity from God), he uses *I* for God, because there is no duality. That *I* represents nonduality.

In Hinduism there is one God, which may be called *Brahman*, Parameshvara, Narayana. In this way, God has several names. Each quality of God is given a name but God is only one.

The creation is within God. It is not separate from God. The creation has pairs of opposites only to maintain balance. So evils are also created by God. There is nothing that is created by itself. If that were the case, then God would not be almighty.

In every country in the world people worship God in their own way. If we don't accept their way, we say, "Oh, they don't know God." But in fact it's not true.

We always need some form to visualize or imagine. God has no name or form but we have given God a name and a form so that we can channel our thoughts toward God. Knowingly or unknowingly, there is always a picture created by the mind. Our language is also a chain of pictures. When we say the sound *A*, we see its picture *A*. In fact the sound and the form of *A* are not related, but that's the way we understand it.

Dear V—,

If God is supposed to be like a human being who is all good, all powerful, and managing the universe, the question *Why is there human suffering?* can't be answered. If God is a supreme energy that creates, maintains, and dissolves this creation then the question doesn't arise because the creation goes through an automatic cycle of birth, growth, decay, and death.

Moreover, one thing that is favorable to one person is unfavorable to another person. For example, the rain favors a farmer and his fields but ruins a potter who left pots outside in the sun to dry. Similarly we cause suffering to each other by seeking our own gain.

Are we not responsible for creating suffering for ourselves by causing anger, hate, jealousy, attachment, and ego? An enlightened person sees human suffering and its cause whereas an unenlightened person sees only suffering.

Wishing you success in your sadhana.

Dear M—,

   Jai Sita Ram.

   When you plant the seed of a tree, it first sprouts with its head bending, like a baby with no ego. The bud grows and strengthens upward. Branches come out. Now it is a tree that stands up to wind, rain, snow, fog, etc., and keeps its ego. The tree starts flowering and then fruits. The tree again starts bending as if saying, "I am offering what I have."

   The same thing happens in human life. Children are helpless. When they grow up, they develop ego. But if they attain spiritual enlightenment they become very humble, kind, compassionate, and loving. The chances of falling into maya increase when a person attains some spiritual enlightenment but still keeps their ego high.

   In a household situation, the wife and husband want to be together in all levels of life. Yes, you are what you are. But you don't know who you are. The first thing is to find out who you are. You are a different person in different situations. You read books and become different. It is all confusing. The best thing is to stop thinking and make the mind calm, then you can see the reality.

   It doesn't make any difference if you use different words from different languages for the word *sugar*. The taste will remain the same. All the different words still mean the same sugar. Rama, Krishna, Jesus, Buddha, Mohammed, etc. are different names for the same God.

   One can't be nonattached just by saying *nonattachment*. Real nonattachment comes after realization of the Self.

But one should practice nonattachment, desirelessness, etc. to purify the mind.

There are various paths, like Hinduism, Buddhism, Christianity, Zen, Taoism, etc. Each path says the same thing in different ways. The main aim is to purify the mind.

If you feel so much love for God, then choose the path of devotion. Sing the name of God, surrender all your actions to God, reject ego, and be humble.

CHAPTER

FOUR

What is Guru?

Dear D——,

There is always an appropriate time for accepting a spiritual path. You want to know who your spiritual teacher is. This is a relationship based on faith, trust, and devotion. If you have faith in a person who is on the spiritual path, whose life is a model for you, whose teachings are acceptable to you, whom you can trust, and for whom you can feel devotion, that person is your spiritual teacher. You can't accept a spiritual teacher by simply registering your name with a sect, community, or religion.

Your second question was *Where do I belong?* The answer is simple. You belong to God. God is one, but accepted in various forms, faiths, and ways. One who understands that God is one belongs to all forms of God.

You should not wait for a teacher, a sect, or a community. Start doing your spiritual practices by prayers, meditations, and developing positive qualities.

Dear M—,

1. The path of enlightenment is simple but we make it hard by our unwanted thoughts, desires, and attachments.

2. Your own Self is the real *guru*. You can project your guru onto any living person whom you believe, trust, and love.

3. A student is a packet of gunpowder and the teacher is a spark. The spark ignites the gunpowder. But if there is no spark in a teacher or there is no gunpowder in a student, it never happens.

4. A poet can visualize an abstract thing and can meditate easily. When the mind develops some kind of emotional trance, the poems manifest by themselves. This is also a kind of meditation that can bring enlightenment.

5. We all carry our past in our present. The past is as vast as an ocean. In your past you could be in the Himalayas, you could be with some high saint, etc. But the past is buried in different incarnations. By making the present clear and peaceful your past will be revealed to you.

6. All knowledge is already in you. Some is active and some is dormant. By the grace of the Lord and by your efforts the dormant knowledge can become active. This is called enlightenment.

7. It's not impossible to attain enlightenment without a teacher. Ramana Maharshi did it without a teacher. You can learn to drive without a teacher but it's wise to learn from a teacher and not take the risk of knocking the car here and there in the process of teaching yourself.

8. Contentment, compassion, and tolerance are the pillars that support the palace of peace.
   Wish you happy and healthy.

Dear W—,

Guru is your own Self, which is projected outside onto a person who is more knowledgeable and capable of teaching. Faith and trust in that person make a relationship of guru and disciple. *Guru* is a Sanskrit term for a teacher. It's good that you have a keen desire to find a guru. Desire manifests the object. Your desire to find a guru will create a guru.

In the beginning an aspirant seeks some support from outside. That support comes from a teacher. When the aspirant starts meditating honestly, then their own Self is revealed in the form of a guru or teacher. The aspirant starts listening to the inner voice and finds the path, which is shown by the voice of the heart.

Wish you happy and success in your search for God.

Dear R—,

I am happy to learn about your thirst for the spiritual path. The teacher and student relationship is based on faith and trust. If there is no faith and trust, the relationship can't be established. People join ashrams, religions, and groups yet when they don't develop faith, they feel deserted.

The spiritual path doesn't need any label. One who is developing positive qualities, one who is serving others with no selfish motive, one who loves God's creation is a spiritual person whether or not the person belongs to any religion, sect, or ashram.

My life is for those who want to walk on the spiritual path.

Dear K—,

Sat guru is your own Self, the *atman*, which is God with-in a person. Yes, sat guru is the one and only one that is the Self.

The guru-disciple relationship is based on faith and trust. The relationship is created by acceptance in the mind. This relationship is broken by rejection. But no one can break the relationship with the Self. The Self is the most pure consciousness in a being. That's why *sat* (pure) is added before *guru*.

The aim of life is to attain peace. The world is a school where we learn about pleasure and pain. The person who shows the path to escape pleasure and pain is a guru. We can learn from different people about it. No one can tell you who is your guru or who should be your guru. It is entirely up to you to choose your own guru or gurus.

Dear L—,

The aim of life is to attain peace. A guru or spiritual teacher teaches how to attain that peace. The teacher and student relationship is based on faith and trust. A guru who is not trusted by the student is not his or her guru in reality. A guru doesn't teach much except how to live in the world with truthfulness, with nonviolence, and with selfless service to others. The guru either presents these teaching in words or through the way they live their life.

Dear V—,

The understanding of love, God, or nothingness can't be taught by words, correspondence, or by reading books, just as sweetness can't be described. A teacher (guru) can only point toward a tree and say, "Look there is a bird sitting on a branch." Their duty is finished and the student's duty begins. He or she tries to see the bird, moves their head up, down, sideways and sometimes asks, "Where is the bird?" The teacher again points a finger and says, "Look straight along my finger." The student finally sees the bird. The act of seeing is within, and one only needs to use their vision in the right manner.

I can only tell you that three things are very important to attain reality. They are tolerance, compassion, and contentment. The method of developing these three qualities is to not harm anyone, including yourself.

Wish you happy.

Dear T—,

The aim of life is to attain peace and happiness. It is hidden in every living being. It is more known to some than to others. But even those who know that the aim of life is to attain peace mistakenly accept sensual pleasures as peace and happiness. The result is more pain and confusion in life.

A teacher is not much of a guide except to show the right path for attaining peace and to point out that another path goes in the wrong direction. In both cases you have to walk by yourself. The teacher's duty is finished after simply pointing out the right path. Some people are very gifted. Their hearts know which path is right and which path is wrong. They are guided by their own hearts. But such a person is one in millions.

Why is a teacher necessary? The answer is that they reduce the aspirant's time researching and experimenting with different paths. You can learn to drive a car without a teacher. But it will take a long time to figure out how to start the car, how to accelerate it, how to steer it, and how to stop it. With a teacher you will learn these in ten or fifteen minutes. Also you will be saved from accidents if the teacher is guiding you.

It's good that you are asking yourself about your aim in life.

Dear G—,

If a teacher, or guru, really wants their student to attain peace, then they will not put any conditions or boundaries around the student. But if the student wants to go on a wrong path, it is the teacher's duty to warn the student.

Faith, devotion, and right aim are the three pillars that hold up the spiritual life. I don't claim that I can give enlightenment. I say that anyone can attain it by their own effort. As long as we are not responsible for cleaning out our own garbage, we carry that garbage with us everywhere we go. No one is going to clean out our garbage for us; we have to do it ourselves.

Understand the bondage in life and then you will know how to free yourself. This understanding comes by regular sadhana. In the world you have to live, eat, sleep, work, laugh, and cry, but in your heart you have to feel the bondage and always be thinking about how to get out of it.

Dear U—,

I don't believe that anyone else can eat for you. When people say, "We will pray for you," or, "We will send you to heaven," I really don't accept it. The priests in all religions make their lives important by showing that they are close to God even though they are no different than other people. If God listens to their prayers, then why can't God listen to the prayers of others?

Three things make prayers successful: faith, devotion, and right aim. For faith, devotion, and right aim you don't need to be a *swami*, monk, *sadhu*, or a priest. It's a relationship of the heart with God.

If a painter asks for comments on his painting and changes the painting according to the suggestions, then one day the painting will be nothing but a pile of colors. Everyone will tell you what to do. It's easy to tell others. You can also tell people what to do. But the hardest thing is doing something in your own life. If you are doing something or trying to do something to improve your life and to attain peace, then you don't need to listen to everyone. You can't do everything in one day. But if you go on practicing your own methods, whether it is prayer, yoga, *Karma Yoga*, or Jñana yoga, some day everything will become right by itself.

Those who climb mountains learn the methods and they practice. They pray to the Lord for success and their faith brings success. It's a simple thing.

Dear N—,

Yes, faith is created by the mind, and that faith in a master makes someone *master*. If one has no faith in a master, then nothing will be attained. It is your faith in the master that gives the capability of learning through the master. Some people have faith in a deity of the master. The deity is made of metal or rock. It has no life but through faith a student can learn. For example, Ramakrishna Paramahamsa had such an experience.

The word *sleep* also represents ignorance. In sleep dreams are real. We feel pleasure, pain, and hunger in our dream but when we wake up, we don't feel the pleasure, pain, or hunger of that dream. The sleep of ignorance is exactly the same. When we attain enlightenment, we don't feel the pleasure or pain of the ignorant stage.

One who serves is a servant. The attitude of a servant is mixed with the attitude of a friend and a parent. A servant serves with love and always thinks about the benefit of his master. Your family is a miniature form of the world. If you serve your family perfectly, you are serving the world.

A monk can hide in a jungle or cave where there are no objects to attract the senses but for a householder there are tests everywhere. A householder is in the middle of all desires and yet tries to put limits on desires in order to attain enlightenment.

One who is a householder should be a householder saint, i.e., try to attain enlightenment.

A householder yogi needs society, money, house, and other items because he or she is responsible for the family.

But he or she can develop nonattachment to these even though they are needed for the family. It's the attachment to the object that is to be avoided and not the object itself.

The ego appears as *I am this* and *I am that*. When the ego is removed, there remains only *I am*, which is the Self unrelated to any name or family.

Dear K—,

I am happy to know that you are doing sadhana.
Sadhana is a part of life. Knowingly or unknowingly we
are all striving to attain God. Just like a child eats food
but doesn't know that he is eating to survive. You have
your family life and also social life. So you have to join
all levels of life together and then work on each level.

> For the spiritual level – sadhana.
> For the household level – job, health, responsibility.
> For the social level – friendship, compassion, etc.

If you only do sadhana and don't pay attention to the
other two levels, you can't keep a balance unless you
renounce the world.

The most important thing is the perfection of aim.
When you are determined to attain God, then all your
work will start channeling toward God. Your garden will
be God's garden. Your hiking will be for God. Your family
will be God's family. The ego of me and mine will disappear. Whether you work for your family or for society does
not make any difference because it is also God's work.

Just as a circus girl performs different acts on a tight-
rope but never makes a misstep that will throw her balance
off, a yogi who has perfection in his aim works in different
levels of life but will never step onto a wrong path.

Your faith in me is your guru. If there is no faith in a
person who is accepted as a guru, then that person is not
the guru.

Dear A—,

I read your letter. I am happy to know that you have been on a spiritual path since 17 years of age.

The purpose of human incarnation is: (1) to experience the world, (2) to achieve liberation or eternal peace. The world is experienced by our ego, mind, intellect, and senses. When we experience the world our desires and attachment get stronger, which brings discontentment and pain. Because we live in pain and miseries in the world, we look for God or eternal peace. Now you can see that the cause of pain and miseries in the world is our own ego, which expresses itself as desires and attachment. So one who wants to attain God (eternal peace) should reduce desires and attachments first, which will automatically reduce the ego.

Disciple and *discipline*—both words come from the same root. A person who observes discipline given by a master is called disciple. What is that discipline that is necessary for a disciple?

1. Always remember your aim, which is to attain peace (God).
2. Develop good qualities in your actions and thoughts, such as honesty, compassion, and love.
3. Be nonviolent.
4. Remember God.
5. Perform selfless service, such as helping the poor, old, sick, or orphaned.

Dear S—,

You asked, "Can you teach me to be simple? Can you help me to look inside? Can you help me crack through fear?"

These things can't be taught. They are developed by reducing ego, attachment, and anger. One can't develop positive qualities without making a discipline in life. First one should develop an aim, which is the attainment of peace. One should move regularly toward that aim.

The next question is how to move. The answer is by removing negativities. Negative attitudes are the obstacles in our journey toward God, peace, universal love (you can use any name).

Attachment to the world is the cause of ego, ignorance, and fear. If one develops nonattachment in the mind in all actions and thoughts, then all problems are solved by themselves.

Dear B—,

Yes, there is an absolute truth that is beyond definition, description, and explanations. We can only say *God*. It's a matter of experience.

As long as the real is not contacted or identified, everything is unreal. Sadhana, worship, and prayers are games, tricks, and plays, but they are very important for finding the truth.

I always love you, whether you feel it or not. You ask about our relationship. It's a relationship of guru and disciple in which all relationships merge. You will know me through sadhana. You can't understand me by seeing my physical body. How the body acts, plays, shows pleasure and pain is an illusion. If I have to know you, I have to see inside you and not your physical body.

My only aim is to bring people into sadhana. For me sadhana is not only asana, pranayama, and meditation. Sadhana includes developing positive qualities, building right conduct, closeness with your parents, friends, and society, right livelihood, etc.

Why are you afraid to talk to me? I saw you once drifting away, confused, and helpless. From that time I always tried to bring you to the right path. Probably you don't know that I told A— to see if you are doing OK. But you did very well. You changed yourself and now you understand what you have to do in the world.

FIVE

Yoga Practice &
Philosophy

Dear G—,

It is always difficult to do sadhana because the mind seeks comfort. In doing sadhana one needs to sacrifice comfort. So you should kick yourself to do sadhana early in the morning. Even the plants, trees, birds, and animals wake up in the morning and make themselves ready to begin the day.

Just as the nature of water is to flow downhill, the nature of a human being is to flow toward laziness and other negative qualities. By yoga practice this downward flow is changed to upward. That is, positive qualities are developed.

Surrendering to God and developing positive qualities are the same thing. Not doing anything, just sitting, is not surrendering to God. Surrendering to God is not identifying yourself as the doer.

It is simple to explain things but very difficult to put them into practice. There are so many scriptures full of good teachings. People read those scriptures but still remain ignorant. The reason is that they don't practice what they read, hear, or learn.

It's good to wake up before the sun rises. In the morning when the sun rises, the breath goes into *sushumna*. If one meditates at that time for only ten to fifteen minutes, it will be more effective than meditating for two to three hours later.

Dear O—,

God is within us. We forget to identify with God because of our ego, which sits in the mind and identifies only with the body. By the regular practice of meditation, the first veil—identifying with the body—is removed. The mind is concentrated in the light or sound of the heart. This creates loss of body consciousness.

When the mind goes deeper, all the senses start following the mind. So the mind loses its power of being master of the senses. This eliminates the ego of the mind. In the third stage, the mind loses its own identity and appears in the form of atman (the Self). Atman is God within a being, and *paramatman* is the supreme God. It's like water kept in several pitchers; the water is all from the same river, but we see it as separate. Paramatman is that river and atman is the water in the pitcher. It's the same water.

Meditation is the key to open the doors. By practicing meditation you can attain samadhi, and by samadhi God is revealed within. Knowing the Self, there is nothing else to be known, because the Self is omnipresent, omniscient, and omnipotent.

Dear D—,

A tree is inside a seed in a subtle form. When the seed is sown, the tree comes out in the gross form. In the same way all knowledge is already in our mind and by doing yoga this knowledge comes out like a tree from a seed.

Just as rich soil in the ground is important for a seed to grow, faith is the ground for yoga to grow. Faith is the real teacher. Faith is real yoga, and faith is real attainment. We project our faith onto some person as a teacher and feel that person's love, peace, and wisdom inside us. If we don't project our faith on that person, then we don't feel anything. They will be just another person.

Though there are millions of methods of yoga, the aim is one and that is to make the mind free from thought waves. For making the mind free from thought waves, meditation is the most important practice.

But it's not easy to meditate because many obstacles interfere. There are two main obstacles. The first is the physical body, and second is the samskaras (impressions of the actions of past births).

Weakness or stiffness in the body, illness, and disease are physical hindrances that can be cured by doing asanas every day.

The obstacles caused by samskaras are very strong. Aspirants are drawn to the wrong path even though they know that they are going the wrong way, yet they can't stop themselves. Things like gambling, drug addiction, and thoughts of hurting others are impurities of the mind. The mind is purified in two ways:

1. Pranayama and meditation.
2. By cultivating positive qualities.

For developing positive qualities, selfless action, satsang, study of scriptures, and reading life histories of saints are important.

If you make a schedule for your daily life based on the above, it will be easy for you to attain enlightenment.

It is said, "Mother and motherland are more than heaven." *Ahimsa* doesn't mean to let anyone beat or rape you. You should defend yourself, but you must not hurt anyone including yourself by words, actions, and thoughts. This is ahimsa.

Wish you happy and success in your sadhana.

Dear R—,

According to yoga a soul goes through many births until liberation is attained. So there is no failure. The only thing we can say is that it takes a longer time or a shorter time to attain liberation.

Again, there is no fixed time for attaining liberation. It's like focusing a magnifying glass with the rays of the sun. When the magnifying glass's distance is fixed, the sun's rays collect in the center and generate heat. The heat burns the straw underneath in no time. The time in meditation is only spent in fixing the mind on one object. As soon as it is fixed, it will burn out all the impurities of the mind and liberation is attained.

If we want to attain something, we put all our energy into it. For example, those who participate in the Olympics or those who climb mountain peaks practice every day. In the same way, if we really want peace and want to overcome the ignorance of this world, we have to practice every day.

There is always fear in everything. But we have to face the fear, fight the fear, and finish it forever.

Dear S—,

I read your letter. Your mind jumps to so many things all at once that you feel burdened, and nothing gets done properly. So create a discipline in your life, like:

Sleeping hours   _____
Sadhana hours   _____
Working hours   _____
Study hours   _____

If a person wants to hike a mountain and starts thinking about how weak they are, how bad their diet is, or how impure their mind is, then that person can't go very far. You have to be positive, enthusiastic, courageous, and firm in your aim.

What is liberation? It's not a place where one goes and sits liberated. It is in this life where all shackles of desire and attachment are removed. You still work in the world. You still eat and sleep but you don't feel attached to anything. Only the liberated person experiences that complete freedom. Others only talk about their imaginary concept of liberation.

Dear I—,

You can do partial silence. At a certain time of day or on certain days of the week, you can practice silence. Reading, writing, and satsang are also important for your self-development.

You had asked about enlightenment. In yoga overestimating oneself is one of the impediments. I had to remove that impediment in you. Also, in comparison to the infinite conscious principle, individual consciousness is always a beginner's stage. Monks live in caves, perform hard austerities for their whole life, and they are still beginners unless they achieve liberation.

My guru gave me very honest teachings. He did not give me any false assurance that he would give me enlightenment, but told me, "It's your garbage and you have to clean it," and, "I can cook for you but can't eat for you." It's a marathon. Whoever goes on running in spite of falling will achieve the goal. Those who stop running will never achieve the goal.

Dear T—,

I am happy to know that you are getting your Ph.D. on meditation. According to tradition, monks are not allowed to write or talk about sadhana. I am sorry I can't give you the information you want about my sadhana. But I can give you a general idea about meditation.

In meditation the breath becomes shallow and smooth. The deeper meditation gets, the more shallow the breath gets and in the state of samadhi the breath is not felt inhaling or exhaling at all. Breathing is a function of *rajas guna* and meditation is a state of *sattva guna*. In the waking and working states, rajas guna predominates so the individual can't meditate and the breath may be long, short, deep, or shallow. All kinds of breathing patterns are mixed.

In meditation the mind takes the form of the object. It dissolves into the object and all other mental activities cease. In that state, the mind attains true knowledge of the object and the mind becomes satisfied, which creates a blissful feeling.

In meditation the flow of the senses working outside stops. The mind is turned inward and the senses follow the mind and turn their activities inward. The ears start hearing inner sounds. The flow of blood and the heart beat make a sound like the buzzing of bees, a waterfall, the sound of a drum, etc. The eyes see an inner light that appears in different colors; a bright golden light may appear. The nose senses a pleasing smell. The tongue notices a good tasting saliva, etc. These things appear in each aspirant differently.

If the mind is not pulled out by the fear of losing the reality of the world, then the mind penetrates several layers of consciousness. Upon emerging from that meditative state an aspirant carries two things: the knowledge experienced and nonattachment to the world.

You have to write on obstructions in meditation because obstructions are also a main part of meditation. They are divided in two categories: general and particular. The particulars are different in different people and you can ask hundreds of meditators about their particular obstructions in meditation. The generals are common to all people in different degrees.

Dear A—,

Jai Sita Ram.

Bondage and freedom are two ends of the same rope. There is no freedom without bondage and vice versa. What is bondage? It's nothing but our desires. Any desire that is active in the mind or that is in our memory is bondage. When the desires are weakened we feel freedom. This freedom can be from a little desire of wanting a car, house, or TV, or the big desire of clinging to life. As long as we are clinging to life we need all worldly desires. So we are binding ourselves with so many ropes.

Freeing ourselves, if we remove one rope at a time, may take years or several births. So, it is better to remove the main cause of bondage, which is clinging to life or the ego to live. This ego is weakened by surrender to God or by understanding our limitations.

Om shanti.

Dear B—,

I received your letter. It is good that you are doing regular sadhana.

All that the mind identifies is still an illusion even if it is a religion, dogma, teacher, or scripture. For attaining liberation, we have to break the boundaries set by the mind. That happens only when we attain samadhi. For one who is honest in sadhana, who has surrendered to God, and who has faith and devotion, neither time, space, nor any environment can stop the progress. Sadhana is a personal thing. It cannot be shared with anyone. Although people live in an ashram and meditate together, they are still always separate in their minds.

My love and Jai Sita Ram to your family.

Dear H—,

There is no other way except to do regular sadhana. In sadhana sometimes we get pleasure and sometimes pain, sometimes love and affection, and sometimes anger and hate. All our samskaras come out like seeds come up when sown in the ground. But when these sprouts are not watered they don't grow any more. The first step is that we have to stop watering sprouts of bad qualities. When all bad qualities are finished then we have to stop watering sprouts of good qualities also. Only then we can attain the stage of *kaivalya* (stage free from all good and bad qualities).

Wish you happy and success. My love and Jai Sita Ram to C—.

Dear O—,

Jai Sita Ram.

The limits of the human mind reach up to the main energy, which is the Supreme. But we can't see up while we are looking down. To see up we have to stop looking down. The higher consciousness, or God or Self (any name can be given), is separate from the lower consciousness, or mind, world, etc. Yoga means union. Union comes after separation. The separation here is between higher consciousness and lower consciousness, or say, the Self and the mind, or God and creation. We mistake the lower consciousness for higher consciousness, the mind for the Self, the world for God. So we don't see any separation and never think of union.

May God bring success to your sadhana.

Dear G—,

The soul is the consciousness within all things. It is the pure essence of all forms. But the soul, which is beyond any actions, beyond death and birth, appears to be doing actions, taking birth, and dying. Actually the soul is living inside the covering of desires and attachment, like an almond stays inside its shell. The soul is covered by maya. Maya means the illusion that is the result of all worldly desires. The world itself is made by desires so the world is also maya. When a person dies their desires take the soul away from the body and then the same desires become a cause of rebirth, the return to a body. When these desires totally disappear, the soul merges into its origin (God). This is called salvation.

By doing yoga sadhana people realize this maya through higher consciousness, and that realization makes them free from maya. In other words, a person gets dispassion for the world because higher consciousness leads to the understanding that the world is illusion or maya.

Every human being in the world thinks about death. The greatest fear in life is death, because people think that after death they are finished forever. But those who think that the body is not their soul (higher consciousness) cultivate a faith that even if the body dies they will not die. This thought creates devotion for God and they believe that their relationship with God is unbreakable. The fear of death disappears.

The parents are the first guru (teacher). Everyone should have love, respect, and devotion for their parents. According to samskara theory, to fulfill desires a person takes birth in a family to which he or she was related in past lives. Since the parents are also connected by the same kinds of desires, the whole family gets pleasure or pain from each other by taking birth together. But some save themselves from this kind of collective pain and pleasure.

To see a flash of light in meditation is always good. There is no difference if you make it or it is actually there, because you can't make a thing that is not actually there. Try to see the light for a longer period.

A cold is a natural process of cleansing the mucous from inside the head. But it should not continue for more than several days. Using mustard powder with your food for a few days will help you in doing pranayama. It will cure the mucous.

Dear A—,

Shaktipat means awakening of *kundalini* by passing spiritual energy. A student becomes enlightened at the very moment of shaktipat. In olden times a guru would select an advanced student who was quite ready for enlightenment and touch their head or *ajna chakra* or give a *mantra*, and the student would become enlightened.

No one can give enlightenment unless the other is ready for it. People develop emotional excitement when they are touched. It is emotional energy that causes them to jerk, twitch, or scream and not the kundalini energy. If a woman wants a man very badly and somehow the man's hand touches the woman, the woman feels as if electricity is passing through her body. It is an energy but not kundalini energy. It's an emotional energy that appears in eight variations called *ashta sattvik vikara*, which are: (1) petrified or stunned, (2) tears, (3) sweating, (4) paleness or redness in the face, (5) horripilation (hair standing on end), (6) trembling, (7) cracking of the voice, and (8) fainting.

These emotions are also shown by dancing, singing, rolling on the ground, crying, twisting of the body, screaming, long breath, ignoring people (attitude of indifference), falling of saliva, horse laughs, hiccups, feeling cold, or twitching in any part of the body.

In the beginning of yoga everyone gets very excited, like a romance, but when yoga becomes an everyday practice, the romance fades away and you have to deal with the reality of your thoughts, desires, and samskaras. A guru can't remove those obstacles. By the regular practice of yoga those obstacles are removed. But everyone seeks an easy, short, comfortable way to attain God. One who wants to compete in the Olympics practices for eight to twelve hours every day. How then can it be easy for a person who wants to attain the highest goal in life?

In India there are thousands of people with Sai Baba everyday. It's a good satsang but it doesn't remove their problems in day to day life. People get sick, angry, and jealous. They try to push others away. At the same time they seek enlightenment. Without purifying our minds we can't attain God.

The question is *How to purify the mind?* The mind is purified by meditation, developing good qualities, and selfless service. One can choose any one, or all three. In fact each one includes the other two.

If you admit the truth, it's very frightening to realize that you have to work hard to attain enlightenment, and even if you do work hard, there is no guarantee that you will get success. So everyone tries to cover up the truth and think that enlightenment is not very far away. It's an encouraging thought but not a true thought.

Those who climb Mt. Everest prepare themselves physically and mentally for years. When they reach base camp, they discuss how they will have to fight for their survival. Some may not reach the top. Some may never return. In this way they accept all the positive and negative possibilities.

In yoga exactly the same thing happens. When you attain the first samadhi, that is your base camp. All kinds of fears come at that point and you have to discuss them within yourself. Then you are ready to continue your journey.

Association with holy people is very important.

A guru can cook for you but can't eat for you.

Dear P—,

Practice your mantra regularly. Try to attain peace in life. Do some physical exercise for the gross body. Do some breathing exercises to purify your mind. Do meditation for attaining liberation.

Life is not a burden. We create burdens by our desires, attachment, and ego. If we accept life in the world, it creates contentment and all conflicts fall away.

Wish you and your husband happy and healthy.

Dear U—,

Instead of suffering on the sea of *samsara*, learn to surf. A surfer can go inside the tunnel of the wave and come out safely. The surfboard for a yogi is made of nonattachment. Nonattachment doesn't mean noncaring, nonloving, or ignoring others. Nonattachment is a mental state. The mind deals with everything in life but always sees everything as unreal. Its reality is only based on ignorance.

In the Kumaon area of India there was a monk who always dressed in western suits and wore kingly turbans. Only a few people knew that he was a Siddha yogi. I'm saying that even if you shave your beard and cut your hair short you are still the same yogi.

Doing satsang with chanting, kirtan, and reading the *Gita* is a very good idea. Gradually you can create a group of spiritually-minded people.

One doesn't fall if one's faith doesn't change. Householders can be great yogis if they have nonattachment. Your fear of falling is baseless as long as your faith does not fall.

Dear J—,

Your daughter asked me to write to you about meditation. Your doubts about meditation are quite natural. It's like a child who sits in an airplane and the airplane goes high up in the sky. The child says, "The airplane is not moving." The child does not feel any kind of movement, but in fact the airplane is moving. The same thing happens in meditation.

Because there is no way to compare whether we are gaining or losing, we don't feel anything in our meditation. But in reality, we gain something by meditation. It is very subtle and we can't feel this gain until perfect peace is attained. Sometimes a little bliss, happiness, and joy come during or after meditation, but it's not the real goal we have to attain. Still, it strengthens faith, and we try to meditate more and more. Similarly, just like a fish that tastes a little bit of worm, comes nearer to it, and finally gets trapped on the hook, the mind tastes the bliss, and perfect peace becomes the trapping of the mind.

Most people think meditation should cure their pain, worries, and fear in one sitting. It doesn't happen unless a person has already developed extreme dispassion. But by sitting regularly, the mind very slowly understands the reality, and the illusion of the world, which is the cause of all pain, goes away.

There are two choices: (1) hide from the pain, or (2) get rid of the pain. Those who hide from the pain try to lean on others. They try to develop false faith in others. They try to close their eyes just like a pigeon closes her eyes when a cat jumps on her. For some time this hiding protects them but in the end they have to come out. At that point, they are very frightened to face the truth of life, which is that we all take birth, grow, decay, and die. Only one percent of people try to stand on their own feet and make themselves ready to face the truth. They don't get frightened by any situation. They accept birth, and they accept death. So, they are not frightened, and they take the responsibility of life fully.

Yoga gives people the strength to stand on their own feet. It develops positive qualities such as contentment, compassion, tolerance, and acceptance every day.

Yoga is not a religion, a sect, or monkhood. Every person does yoga in some way. But when people are not aware of their actions, then it works very slowly. In olden times the enlightened people created the methods of yoga (which are natural in human beings) so that people would develop awareness of their actions and thus attain enlightenment.

Dear Babaji,

Will you teach me how to meditate? Also, I want to know how to get animals to eat out of my hand.

A— (a four year old)

Dear A—,

Yes, I will teach you how to meditate. Close your eyes and see a light inside your head. This is a light of God. Don't think about anything else. Only think about the light.

Animals are afraid of people. People hunt animals for fun. People kill animals, birds, and fish to eat. So the animals are afraid. If someone tries to hurt us, we are also afraid of that person.

Animals will come to you if you don't hurt them, and don't even think of hurting them. Then they will come to you and eat out of your hand.

Dear L—,

In the *Yoga Sutras*, Patañjali has described the obstacles
in sadhana and how to remove them. But we really can't
make rules about obstacles in the subtle stages. One person starts sadhana as a result of pain and misery while
another person starts because of dispassion or devotion.
In these different conditions the obstacles will be different. If one is meditating to get a Ph.D, the obstacles will
be entirely different.

I started meditation as a result of dispassion. I had no
problem with obstacles except sicknesses. After pranayama I would go straight into deep meditation. But I
know people complain that their mind runs around and
sometimes they get strange thoughts that they never
imagined. For a sadhu living in a secluded place who is
not around worldly objects and has no worldly desires,
meditation is simple and straightforward. The sadhu sits
and does a few methods that have been given to him and
then the mind starts withdrawing from outer objects. It
happens because the mind has no desire to satisfy in the
outer world.

For householders who work in the world and have their
family, property, and fame, the obstacles are created by
their attachments. Thoughts of family, money, and fame
will come in various ways. Physical obstacles are the same
for everyone but a nonattached sadhu is bothered less than
others. Obstacles created by samskaras are the strongest
obstacles. Even a dispassionate sadhu can be drawn into
a situation where the mind starts having worldly desires.

Several yogis, monks, and sadhus do hard sadhana for years and all of a sudden one day they desire to be a householder. I met a sadhu who had many siddhis and lived in a cave in a forest. He could heal people's sicknesses. Once a young woman who had tuberculosis came to him to get healed. He allowed the woman to live close by in a hut. The woman was healed but the sadhu fell in love with her. His desires forced him to marry the woman. It was a samskarik obstacle. Samskarik obstacles are different. There is no cure for them except to do regular sadhana, which purifies the mind and burns old samskaras.

Dear T—,

Sadhana is like a dam to stop the flow of water. If the dam gets a small crack, the water starts running out and makes the crack larger and larger. If the dam is made strong and checked all the time, there can't be a crack.

You started disciplining yourself: you stopped smoking, stopped eating meat, and stopped sleeping and eating too much. All of a sudden the desire to smoke came up and you could not overcome this desire. It was the first crack in the dam. When your mind lost the battle against smoking cigarettes, it lost its will power.

You can regain your self-discipline. Losing once in the battle doesn't mean that you can't win again. Eating unfertilized eggs is the same as drinking milk. Eggs are a heat-creating food, so they are avoided in yoga sadhana by those who live in hot places. If six hours sleep makes you weak, sleep for eight hours—10:00 PM to 6:00 AM. You will still have enough time to do things.

Smoking cigarettes is not very good for those who do pranayama. It harms the lungs. By doing sadhana regularly, will power builds up. It is through will power that one is able to do hard austerities. So the first thing is to do sadhana every day in the morning. Gradually the mind will accept the discipline of doing sadhana and then will accept other disciplines.

At present do only the four purification exercises. You can increase the numbers of each exercise. After the four purification exercises do meditation and then asanas. When this schedule gets set after three months, gradually add some more methods.

Dear M—,

I understand your problem from your letter. You tried to understand yourself, your problem, and others but you did it in an imaginary way. You imagined yourself and others in a positive way so that you would feel better. It's like eating candy in a dream. One tastes it and feels good, but then awakens and realizes *I did not eat candy.*

You were in the Institute and probably joined several psychological, yogic, and other workshops there. But your problem was not solved. Theoretically, I could also say, "Love yourself, love others, and all your problems will go away." But how? You can't love anyone, including yourself, if love is not created within. If you do, it will be pretending and that will cause a feeling of guilt and inferiority.

When a lamp is lit, it spreads light by itself. Anywhere you put it, it will give off the same light. Bright objects will shine in this light and dark objects will not shine. When a person develops love, everyone around that person begins to shine (their love begins to come out). So our first duty is to create love within. The methods are meditation and developing positive qualities. Also doing pranayama purifies all 72,000 subtle nerve channels. It takes time. One should practice these methods every day and try to develop tolerance, compassion, and contentment in daily life.

We are our samskaras (past tendencies). We are carrying many past lives in the present life in the form of samskaras. That's why it is so difficult to dig out the problems. But if you can make the negative samskaras weak, then automatically the positive samskaras will emerge.

Samskaras can be weakened by purifying the body and the mind by yogic methods. As I said before, *it takes time*. One who is determined to attain peace will work on yoga every day and face all hindrances patiently.

I suggest that you meditate even if you feel it's difficult to sit, to stop thoughts, and to concentrate. The mind always revolts. If you don't accept defeat, then some day you will see that you've won. You will attain peace, which is love, God, and truth.

Om shanti.

Dear D—,

It's good that you are building a boat. It's a good thing to make new things. But it's not right to worry about the boat all the time. You know nothing can be everlasting. The boat will get old some day or some day you will get detached from it.

The mind doesn't accept sadhana because it doesn't see any physical gain from doing sadhana. If sadhana paid $50 per hour, then everyone would do it willingly. The mind always makes excuses for not doing sadhana. "Oh, I have work to do. Last night I went to sleep late and I should sleep longer. I am tired. Not today, tomorrow for sure, etc." These excuses never end. We make time for all the worldly things but make no time for sadhana, which is the most important thing in life. But we do like its results, which are peace, happiness, and enlightenment.

Making a boat can give you some satisfaction for some time but you need to dwell on eternal peace, which can only be attained by sadhana.

My love and Jai Sita Ram to your family.

Dear C—,

It will be good for you to get your masters degree in Asian Studies. You are a young man, intelligent, and in sound health. It is your time to get an education and learn things. If this time is wasted in sitting around then life becomes harder in the future.

Anyone can die at any time. In the *Ramayana* it is written, "Loss, gain, birth, death, fame, and infamy are all in the hands of God." Two people start the same business in the same town. One succeeds and one fails. Fame and infamy are the same. No one can take birth by choice and no one can choose the time of death.

Death is a part of life. People don't like to think that someday they have to die. They want to forget this part of life. One who accepts death as a part of life is not afraid of death. After fifty years of age the Hindu system recommends *van prastha*, renouncing the world. The main renunciation is to renounce the attachment to life.

The power of kundalini is experienced in different ways. Those who are emotionally predominant feel it in their emotions and those who are intellectually predominant feel it in their knowledge. Some people claim that their kundalini is awakened but they are still in pain, with worries and attachments to the world. In fact they feel emotional energy and think it is kundalini energy. When kundalini is awakened, two things are achieved: 1) dispassion for the world, and 2) knowledge of reality. If these two things are not gained, then kundalini is not awakened, even if people claim their kundalini is awakened.

There is no time limit for awakening kundalini. It can happen at any time. That's why regular sadhana is very important. After acquiring one-pointedness in sadhana one can use any object for focus that the mind likes. All objects that are chosen for concentration are in ajna because ajna is the concentrator and the seat of Om. Om is the indicator of *Ishvara* or Paramatman, the supreme *I-sense*. So if one sticks to Om, it is a direct path.

Samyama develops when sadhana is purified. Samyama is not a difficult thing once you attain samadhi. One can lose samyama after attaining it by not practicing. People attain samyama and lose it when their sadhana gets loose.

If *I* leave this body, the *I* will guide *you*. *I* and *you* will always remain existing.

Dear G—,

When the mind changes its course, i.e., going in instead of going out, the first vision comes as a flash of white light. The mind dissolves in that light and when it comes back to its former state, it brings two things: (1) peace and (2) a sense of the worthlessness of the outer world, or you can say *dispassion*.

When a person who is not yet matured in that state gets such visions, it causes a problem of not being able to adjust to family life or to society. If you want to understand how the mind acts in yogic life, then you should read the *Yoga Sutras of Patañjali*.

First, the mind awakens from its deep sleep (ignorance) and then it is pulled right back. In this way a person goes back and forth for a long time. By regular practice of meditation one can overcome these fluctuations and become established in the state of samadhi.

Dear K—,

Brahman plus maya equals Ishvara, and Brahman plus *avidya* equals jiva, or say pure consciousness plus illusion equals the universal Self, and pure consciousness plus ignorance equals the individual self.

Yes, there is one *purusha* and also there are several purushas. For example there is a lake and you fill several pitchers with its water and then you give them separate names, i.e., lake water and pitcher water. In reality the water in the lake and in the pitcher are no different. Separate identity arises only because water is in the pitcher.

About rebirth: We are in three bodies but only the gross body is visible. This gross body dies and never takes rebirth. Inside the gross body is an energy body or subtle body. It doesn't die but becomes a seed when the gross body dies. That seed is carried away by the samskaras (the laws of nature) into space. When that seed finds favorable soil, it starts germinating (rebirth).

Yes, the pitcher is an ego in a gross sense. That ego, which is the notion *my body*, is removed at the time of death. You can see that the pitcher also goes through transformations. It may break into pieces. It may burn to ashes. It may wash away in a flood, etc. All these changes are *karmas* of that pitcher. Those karmas finish when the five elements that constituted that pitcher are separated and dissolve into their original cause. This is the story of the gross body.

The story of the subtle body is similar but on a subtle level. The subtle body goes through a rebirth process, taking different gross bodies in different spaces and times until the subtle body attains enlightenment. You can say enlightenment is the death of the subtle body.

The causal body, which is the cause of this creation, goes back to its source, which is *mula prakriti*, after the subtle body is liberated. In this way the three bodies are liberated at different times.

Wishing you happy and healthy.

Dear N—,

God is not a religion. God has no name or form. God is a limitless, ever-existing energy. God is within us and everywhere in the world. The question is how to contact that energy or God. There are different ways:

By developing positive qualities the mind is purified.
  When the mind is purified, it starts seeing the truth.
  That truth gives a feeling of God.
By faith, devotion, and yoga practice the mind is purified.
By regular meditation the mind is purified.
By chanting mantras, prayers, and worship the mind is
  purified.

You can make a schedule of your spiritual practice:

1. Do some pranayama breathing exercises and then simply breathe deeply for 4–5 minutes.
2. Sit with the spine straight and watch your breath with closed eyes. When you inhale or exhale, the mind should follow the breath. Or visualize a full moon disk inside your forehead. Do this for 10–15 minutes.
3. Chant some prayers or sing some spiritual songs.
4. Do some physical exercises, such as asanas. If you don't know any asanas, then do some jogging.

After three or four months you will become addicted to these practices and then you can learn advanced practices.
  Wishing you happy and healthy.

Dear P—,

Jai Sita Ram.

I received your letter. I am very happy to learn from you all that the yoga retreat was full of bliss. Yes, Baba Anand Dass is a very good yogi. He is full of love.

To cry in meditation is always good. It purifies the mind and increases devotion. There are eight kinds of *sattvik* emotions. These emotions are a natural process of purification. Actually, these emotions are a method of yoga.

Don't worry about undesired thoughts sneaking into meditation. If any thought comes, don't dwell on it and it will disappear. If you try to stop these thoughts, they will only come more.

Do less pranayama but do it regularly. To do irregular pranayama is not good. Regular and little sadhana is more effective than irregular and big sadhana.

It's good to do arati. It creates love for God. For arati one should wear clean clothes, or one should keep a separate dress for arati.

When you have accepted R— once then always be with him. When water is poured in water, then both waters become one and can't be separated.

Jai Sita Ram to R—. Wish you both happy and successful in life.

Dear B—,

Jai Sita Ram.

In seclusion *Ram puja* is the main thing. You can read the *Ramayana* also.

The main purpose of seclusion is to cut off the outer world, to experience that stage when you are no more in the world. It can't be explained; it is only experienced. That's why seclusion sadhana is practiced.

Until the reality is experienced, the mind always creates self-doubts. Just do your sadhana. It's like climbing a cliff. While a person climbs a mountain, there is only one thing in the mind, which is how to climb up. Sometimes the foot slips but the person carefully brings the foot back. The desire to climb up is so intense that the person does not dwell on the past.

Regular sadhana with faith and devotion is the way to attain the goal.

Dear J—,

Medicine is to cure the disease and if it makes the disease worse, then it should not be taken. A spiritual center is for attaining mental peace and if one gets more pain there, then one should change their pattern of living.

The younger generation needs your help. How many boys and girls are developing confusion and running aimlessly here and there? You can understand the cause of their confusion and can help them. For this you need your own place. When you can teach them Zen meditation or other yoga techniques, you need not be dependent on ashrams or teachers. It stops the spiritual growth of the student. In India the yoga tradition was that after learning methods a student would leave that place and practice according to the instructions of the teacher. The teacher would say, "A small tree can't grow under a big tree."

To understand samskaras, it is first just as difficult to understand thought waves. Roughly we can say that the print of actions upon the mind are samskaras. But, according to the theory of rebirth, one gets prints in their mind from the previous births, so those prints are also samskaras. They are in layers and can be pealed off by meditation or spiritual life.

Samadhi is the only way by which these samskaras, which are the cause of birth, can be wiped out completely, and that brings salvation. When a child is scared in childhood, he or she develops a habit of becoming fearful. When the child grows up, the fear remains. But it can go away if he or she is forced to face some difficult situations or becomes dispassionate.

The root of all fear is death (losing the body or losing the pleasures of the body). It has innumerable branches. In fact, all desires are its branches. So no one is free from fear. It remains in every single being to greater or lesser degrees.

There are many fears, including the desire for name, fame, and money, and the attachment to people or society. One who is beyond these things doesn't get fear. In Sanskrit it's called *nir-dvandva-avastha*. When everyone is in the same trap, one person should not consider him or herself as weak, but instead should strive bravely to get out of the trap.

After the *bandhas* are perfected, all pranayamas become easy. Now you can do some pranayamas, which you should learn in person from a teacher.

Dear C—,

There are millions of methods but the aim is one. A medicine that cures a sickness is taken until the sickness is gone.

Asanas and pranayamas are for developing meditation. When we climb a mountain we carry a stick for a support, but the stick becomes a burden when we reach the top. Similarly, asana and pranayamas are not needed when samadhi is perfected.

Mantra yoga is another system to attain the same goal. There are millions of mantras in different languages and religions. The aim is the same. There is no difference whether you drive a car, take a bus, or fly to New York. It will be the same New York when you get there, but the means of arriving are different. Different means suit people of different temperaments.

There is no separation or conflict if one is honest to oneself. Do *japa* with il-rahim, hung-sah, so-hum, Om, or Lord Jesus Christ have mercy upon my soul.

Everything will go to the same melting pot. Om is a good mantra because it doesn't belong to any particular religion. It's the sound of creation, and it indicates the Lord.

Dear S—,

Yoga is a very big word. People think yoga means asanas and pranayama. In fact the desire to attain God and any action to attain God is yoga. There are millions of paths to attain God, peace, knowledge, reality. Although the ways are different, the ultimate aim is the same.

Your question is how to channel the energy that you store and that needs to be used properly. In the *Bhagavad Gita*, the practice of Karma Yoga, or selfless work, is mentioned. You can work in a nursing home, or you can help elderly people or single mothers who are unable to fix their houses or gardens. You can work with little kids. If it is not possible due to your circumstances, then make money and give to the poor. In this way you will use your energy without getting attached to any work, person, place, or thing.

We classify spiritual people in two classes: renunciates and householders. Renunciates withdraw from the world as much as they can until they achieve enlightenment. They observe celibacy. They live in seclusion. They do hard austerities, etc. People who are not in this category should consider themselves as householders even if they are not married or living with someone because there remains the desire to be a householder some day. A yogi of this category should contact people, give love and affection, observe social rules (that do not harm sadhana), and at the same time keep a limit on desires.

For a householder yogi the best thing is to get married and consider the family as a world. Such a person should take care of his or her world honestly and peacefully, with devotion and faith in God. A person who can fix the parts of a toy locomotive engine can also fix the big engine because the machinery is the same. In the same way one who is successful in taking care of a household world is capable of taking care of the big world.

You wrote, "If yoga is not for me. . . " You have faith and devotion to God, so how can you separate yourself from yoga? In one whose aim is to attain God, all his or her actions become yoga. Anything he or she does is to attain God.

Do your sadhana every day and be happy.

Dear Y—,

You want peace. Everyone wants peace. Peace can't come by itself nor can it be purchased or given by someone. You have to work hard to attain peace. People do yoga to attain peace. Yoga is not only postures and breathing exercises. We have to cultivate positive qualities in our day-to-day life. Life is not coming, but going. Every single second is flying away from our lives. If we are not trying to attain peace, then we have lost, are losing, and will lose the precious seconds, minutes, hours, days, and years of our lives.

CHAPTER

SIX

Life & Death

Dear L—,

Jai Sita Ram.

If a person thinks the burden of the world is on their shoulders, they feel the weight of the world and in a few years they become hunchbacked. Then one day the person sees clearly outside and realizes that the world exists by itself, but it's too late. The hunchback cannot be straightened.

You have your duties and responsibilities to the world and you can do them with a smile on your face or you can have a sad heart and tears in your eyes. It doesn't make any difference to the world but it makes a difference in the way you feel.

Ninety percent of pain is self-inflicted. It can be removed by understanding that there is no real cause of pain.

What is perfection? Perfection for each person is different. You draw a line and it is perfect for you. But an artist doesn't see it as perfect and draws another line and sees that as perfect. A person with a magnifying glass comes and sees that the line is thick in one place and thin in another and says it is not perfect.

The blade of a sword can be so perfect that no one can deny it. But if you see that same blade under a microscope, you will see that it looks like a mountain chain.

A person can't love anyone if love is not developed inside of them. It's like trying to show light with an unlit candle. To develop love one should stop hating people including one's self.

The silkworm makes a net to imprison itself. In the same way a person makes a net of attachments, desires, and possessiveness, and sits inside that net in pain and depression. As long as this net is not broken, the silkworm remains dormant. But as soon as it is broken, the silkworm emerges in a new form: a butterfly that can fly and that makes everyone happy. So break the net of your attachments and be free.

Wishing you happy and healthy.

Dear K—,

Jai Sita Ram.

I understand your inferiority complex. It can be cured if you try to overcome it. But most people like the pain of a thorn in their foot.

The yoga methods you did, i.e., sound, nectar, word, etc., are also in *Ashtanga Yoga*. Ashtanga Yoga is a vast subject. It's not only postures and breathing exercises.

Before doing yoga, you have to make up your mind that you don't want to live in the confusion of your thoughts, which cover your mind like a tangled web of barbed wire.

I don't tell people to do asanas and pranayamas, but I do say that these practices help a person to improve their health, clear their mind, and attain peace. It takes a long time to get peace—at least three years of regular practice. Very few people can stick to it.

The next thing is to open yourself by playing, singing, dancing. In the beginning people are afraid to do it, but once they come out of their shells they can do it. It cures their inferiority complex very fast.

What is guilt? For how long does guilt remain? The feeling of guilt is a good hideout for people who have an inferiority complex. They tell themselves that they feel too guilty to be with others, and by this pretext they separate themselves from others and enjoy their pain. This becomes the pattern of their life, which, in its advanced stage, cripples them in society. The same kind of people also use yoga as a hideout. They live separately and think they are doing yoga, but in fact they don't do yoga. They simply sit in a corner where no one can see them.

You can get out of your shell. It's no problem. Change your life pattern. Forget about your past and the feelings of guilt. It is all created by your mind. No one thinks you are guilty of anything. Your mind can wipe out this feeling. There is no mantra, drug, or posture that can cure it. You have to break the pattern by yourself.

At the retreat there were several people who had the same problem. They tried to get out of their shell. They started jumping and playing, and they changed.

It will not be healed by talking. You will go on talking, making everything painful. It will never end. You have to break the pattern. Join clubs. Play physical games. Sing and dance. Don't feel guilty when you do these things.

Dear D—,

No one knows what will happen in four or five years, but the world functions on hope. You have to think positively to get encouragement.

It's good that you and G— are getting along well. Problems always come in relationships. If the problems are not solved, then it causes anger, hate, and jealousy to form in the mind. The human mind is full of desires. It's not like an animal mind, which is set and limited. The human mind can think of various ways of getting pleasure and happiness, and in the process of getting pleasure it creates pain in other areas.

A therapist can help to some extent but without using your own understanding, outer help can't solve the problem forever.

Yes, I met your children this summer. They are both very good children. Both are intelligent and healthy. I believe in discipline. Without discipline we can't progress. If a child is disciplined from an early age, then it becomes the child's nature.

I think people separate themselves by developing the nature of comparison and competition. But without competition one can't progress. Sometimes a person loses a game and then stops playing all games. It eliminates the pain of losing but creates the pain of separation. No one wins everything all the time. But some don't get overwhelmed by the pain of losing and they try again and again. These kind of people become friends of everyone.

Another cause of separation is projecting our pain, anger, and hate onto others. Our mind doesn't want to accept that it is our fault. It always tries to prove that our pain is caused by someone else. If we think honestly about it, then we realize that the main cause is our own projection. We expect something, we desire something, and when it doesn't happen, we project our emotions in a negative way.

I don't like limitations in the social environment. One should expand their social life in order to attain more knowledge of the world. Spiritual groups set limits and don't want to see outside of those limits. It develops fanaticism, which is not good for society.

Wish you happy and success.

Dear T—,

Jai Sita Ram.

Don't separate yourself from social activities, but do your sadhana regularly. The world is an abstract art. Every one sees it as they want to see it. It is a garden of roses and it is also a forest of thorny bushes and poison oak.

You don't need to stop seeing your friends to seek the truth. You have to seek the truth in everything, including your friends, family, and society.

The real hermit is one who plays in the world just like a child plays with toys and leaves them scattered on the ground when he is finished playing.

Don't make yourself lonely and also don't break the limit of your desires. God is beyond name and form. God is in everything and that is the truth. When the truth is revealed by the mind and an aspirant begins to feel it, then he or she becomes enlightened.

Dear J—,

A livelihood is earned in various ways. Any work we do, if we do it honestly and without hurting anyone, is right livelihood. But one should know that if a horse makes grass his friend, then he will die hungry. When a farmer plows the ground, several worms and insects get killed. If you think farming is not right livelihood, then you can't eat food.

We don't need to go so deep in thinking about life in this world. We do have to be honest in our mind, actions, and words. It's enough.

Do your sadhana regularly and don't worry about the past, which has already passed, or the future, which is unknown. Only remain in the present with your mind peaceful and be happy.

Dear B—,

Desires, attachment, and ego: these three are the cause of dissatisfaction in life. But without them we can't live in the world. So, we can only be happy if we put limits on desires and attachment.

Money doesn't make anyone happy. It brings more worries, fear, and greed. You worry about the future, but you don't know what will happen in the future. The most important thing is the present. If you make the present peaceful, then you don't need to go into your past and you don't need to worry about your future.

The present is made peaceful by acceptance. Not accepting the present creates discontentment. You want to earn lots of money, which means that you don't accept your present earnings. It creates dissatisfaction.

What happened in the past can't be altered. You go to a psychologist and talk about it, and somehow you accept that you have forgiven others and feel better. If we do sadhana regularly, we automatically remove the past and only think of the present.

Dear G—,

Jai Sita Ram.

No one has ever been fully contented by pursuing desires. Rich men are hankering after wealth and property. Lustful people are running after sensual objects. It's a mirage. Go on chasing it and you will find nothing.

Your restlessness is based on your imaginary idea that there is something better out there. Romantic life is not a reality. It is a momentary life. No one can live a romantic life forever. Some of the best actors and actresses have committed suicide. Their romantic life became a curse for them, whereas someone living a simple life rarely commits suicide.

Your desire is to live life to the max. What is the max? How do you measure it? Isn't the max a rainbow? You look for the rainbow and when you reach there the rainbow is still seen way ahead. The desire for the max will not end. Time will run away in desiring. One day the senses will not be able to enjoy the world and still the desire for more will remain. The body gets old and the world dumps old people in homes. They cry out for love and support but no one is there to hear them.

We see it everywhere but we forget that this is the fruit of having run after more and more colorful desires. Expectation is your problem. Your dreams are your problem. You live in your desires and your imagination. When they do not manifest you get restless.

The world is a race course. Everyone is running. One who starts looking at the spectators trips and falls. No one waits for the fallen runner.

ॐ

Dear R—,

This is life. It includes pleasure, pain, good, bad, happiness, depression, etc. There can't be day without night. So don't expect that you or anyone will always be happy and that nothing will go wrong. Stand in the world bravely and face good and bad equally. Life is for that. Try to develop positive qualities as much as you can.

Dear A—,

As long as you are not completely recovered from the weakness, take rest. The body is a temple of atman (God).

Sick are those who do not worship God. You have faith and devotion to God so you are not sick. The gross body's nature is to take birth, grow, decay, and die. This happens to everyone and no one can deviate from that cyclic order. But for those who stick to the hub (God), their circle is smaller.

My love and Jai Sita Ram to you and your yoga family.

Dear P—,

I heard that your cancer is progressing. In this worldly
reality you carried your responsibilities carefully and
completely. Now the functional body is becoming non-
functional. It's only in the gross body. The subtle body,
which holds the soul like a baby in its lap, never ceases
to exist. If you think deeply about that inner baby all the
time you will not feel alone. That inner baby is the God
within.

The aim of life is to attain inner peace. Money can't
buy it. No one can give it to others. It is achieved by one's
own clear understanding. Free yourself from the past
memories and future expectations. Just sit with that baby
in the present, contented, and in peace.

Dear M—,

Nonacceptance of life causes discontentment and that is pain. If we accept ourselves as we are and surrender to God, then we will love everyone including ourselves. Life has four stages: birth, growth, decay, and death. Everyone who takes birth will pass through these four stages. If we understand and accept this, then we will not be afraid of life.

It is our own fear that stops us from accepting and loving others. We get the same reaction from others in return. If we break this fear and accept everyone, then everyone will also react in the same way in return.

Wish you happy.

Dear V—,

Don't torture yourself by creating nonacceptance of yourself. You are a householder and it is your duty to take care of the family. It has nothing to do with divine consciousness within you. Decondition your mind from the belief that you are separated from God, that you are guilty, a sinner, etc. Think that you are a liberated being who is doing your duties in the world as an instrument of God. You can't be a sinner if you think you are simply an instrument of God.

Isn't it a matter of deconditioning? Air inside a balloon is the same universal air. In the same way, the same universal consciousness is within you. Just identify with it.

Dear C—,

Jai Sita Ram.

No one in the world is perfect. We get good and bad habits in two ways: (1) Samskaras or the impressions of actions from past lives. It's very difficult to have any control over such habits unless we build up very strong will power by doing hard austerities. (2) Environment. This includes everything from when babies are in the womb and get the emotions of the mother to when they grow up and copy their parents, neighbors, friends, and the rest of society.

The second type of habit is not difficult to break. As soon as we understand that this habit is wrong, we stop it. If a habit formed by samskaras is bad, then it's very dangerous.

For example a person loves killing. Inside his mind he knows killing is bad but he loves killing. It gives him pleasure. He cannot stop it because he is guided by his samskaras. By wrong actions he builds more samskaras, and in this way descends to an animal level.

There is one thing about you that is disturbing your life, which is, you are hiding yourself from your childhood. To hide one lie we have to lie a hundred times. All your energy is used in hiding. In fact, you don't like hiding and this creates much pain in you.

You don't want to accept that you are hiding. Because one part of you is very strong and commanding. This comes out only when you see that there is no one who can challenge you. As soon as you feel threatened by someone, you try to retreat from your position and you blame others for your retreating.

You can utilize your energy in a right way by not hiding. There is no use hiding. It causes pain. It creates fear. It deprives you of your strength. If you stand in front of others openly, you will find all your problems are gone.

Dear N—,

If you offer food to a guest who doesn't accept it, you have to take back the food. In the same way if you curse a person and they don't accept it, then the curse will go back to you. You are not outside of the world. The whole world is also inside you. This is because the world is our own projection. So you curse yourself when you curse the world.

On the other hand, if you appreciate the beauty of the world, nature, people, plants, and animals, it can create a feeling of love for everyone.

Good and bad are only a creation of our own mind. If we make an ugly picture of the world in our mind, then we see the world as ugly. So why not make a beautiful picture of the world that provides love, happiness, and peace.

If you want to love and be loved, then don't hate anyone including yourself.

Wish you happy.

Dear J—,

Your question is *Why do we fight?* The answer is simple: *For existence.* We want to make a safe place for ourselves. We need food. We need family. We want to be better than others. So we compare ourselves and try to compete. This nature of comparing and competing creates anger, hate, and jealousy. We are not satisfied by anything. If we have something, we desire more. If we don't have something then we fight to get it. One who is desireless and contented with whatever comes is never jealous, angry, or hateful.

Dear R—,

Comparison and competition are natural tendencies in a human being. All fights, wars, and religious disagreements are based on comparison and competition. At the same time human progress is based on comparison and competition. People try to be better than others and so they work hard. Comparison and competition are painful because they develop discontentment, anger, hate, and jealousy. So progress in a human being is accompanied by pain. The more we are progressing in the world, the more we are discontented. Those people who really accept life as it is, those who have faith in God, and those who work in the world for God can progress without any competition and comparison.

Dear U—,

Anger is a defense mechanism against fear. People who have a lot of fear always defend themselves by getting angry. There is only one proven method to remove anger and that is not to defend your ego. It is very hard not to defend your ego. Only those people who surrender to God can do it.

You can practice:

1. Developing positive qualities.
2. Not getting attached to objects.
3. Reducing your worldly desires.
4. Meditation.
5. Being honest to yourself.

Dear T— (a 5 year old who asked about magic),
Jai Sita Ram.

There are different kinds of magic. One magic is what magicians show to the public. They have several tricks. They can work so fast that our minds can't see the movement. We can see only what they want to show us.

Another magic is to have some mental power, like to know someone's thoughts, or to move things by will.

The highest magic is to become like God. Everyone feels love, happiness, and peace around a person who becomes like God. That person doesn't try to make someone happy or sad. Love surrounds him and spreads out like a light around a lit candle.

In all these kinds of magic we have to practice concentration. If we can concentrate well we can learn the first kind of magic very easily. We can learn the second kind of magic by developing our will. The third kind of magic is attained by purifying the mind.

Try to meditate by looking at an object without blinking for two minutes every day.

Dear P—,

There is nothing wrong in wanting material things when you are a householder. But when you want material things and at the same time reject spiritual life, that is not good.

You want to be a writer but you don't write. Simply wanting can't make you a writer. Desire and effort should go together.

Money has its place in life. It's not the most important thing to have money. With lots of money you can't eat more than the capacity of your stomach. You can't wear several sets of clothes. You can't ride in three or four cars at the same time. Money gives material satisfaction and at the same time dissatisfaction. But you need money to pay all your family expenses.

The most important thing is peace. Without peace, one can't get contentment. Without contentment life is unhappy and miserable.

The body dies and never takes rebirth. The soul and samskaras don't die. Actually you are your soul and samskaras, and not your body. After death your samskaras will carry your soul and take another body. Physically you will not be the same person but internally you will.

We are in the world. We have to desire the things we need. But in desiring the world we should also desire to get out of the world.

Sadhana is very important. It does not matter what sadhana you do. The important thing is to do it regularly.

Wish you all happy together.

Dear U—,

I understand your pain about your son's death. The closest relationship in the world is that of mother and child. All other relationships are formed outside in the world but the relationship of a mother and child is formed inside the mother's own body, which makes them physically and emotionally connected.

Although we all know that one who dies can't come back, we still feel the pain of separation from our beloved ones. But memories of the past never remain the same. Each year the memory of those who are separated gets fainter.

Birth, growth, decay, and death is the cycle of nature. We all have to go through this cycle. No one can be saved from this cycle. But our mind is so confused in the world that we see others going through that cycle and never realize that we are also in the same boat. We cry for others; we lament for others. We show compassion but we do not try to accept that birth, growth, decay, and death together are called life.

Your son came to you to fulfill some samskarik dues and then he left. Who knows whether a great soul came to this earth to complete his last cycle. You are in pain because of your attachment to the physical body of your son. You don't know if the soul in that body was more important on some other level of existence.

Pray for the peace of the departed soul.

Dear J—,

Jai Sita Ram.

This life is full of pain. The pain ends when the mind doesn't relate to the world as *my* and *mine*. We do sadhana as a means to attain peace. There is not just one way. If you can't sit because of pain, do japa, sit on a chair, or lie down. Keep your mind calm.

Defeatism always comes along the way, but we get up and try again. Sadhana is a matter of mind. Three things are needed: Devotion to God, nonattachment to the world, and firm aim. Positive living is the most important. Without a positive mind, pranayama and *dhyana* are mechanical, and don't work. The main thing is to develop love, compassion, honesty, and truthfulness.

Surrender to God's plan and everything will be OK. Surrender is also a way to get dispassion. If you really surrender it is the faster way. You have to accept that there is nothing that you can do. Then, surrender to your samskaras and accept your limitations. It is a test. There are some karmas that we have no freedom to change except by how we react. They are bearing fruit. Lose $100 and get miserable, or lose $100 and don't care. Either way, you have to lose $100.

By accepting your samskaras, gradually a feeling of faith will develop. Faith develops by dispassion and nonattachment. God is not responsible for our pains. It's our samskaras. Both Ramakrishna Paramahansa and Maharshi Ramana died very painful deaths. The body has its own karma. If we relate the body's pain and pleasure with God then we have to lose faith whenever there is pain. When pain is not accepted, it brings attachment, sorrow, and all sufferings. When it is accepted, then it is an austerity. If we face everything in life with the aim of finding peace and accept it as a part of liberation, then it becomes easier. It can change your life.

Once I was sick; I could not sit, no one was there. I had to drag myself to get water. God gives that strength and faith. Sadhana is for developing faith, but pain can also develop that faith. Pain brings an understanding that we are limited beings. So it reduces our ego and develops more surrender.

But there is also a great pull from the world; if there is no pain, or if it gets less, the ego returns to its place. So once you understand your limitations, don't forget them. When there is pain there is more time to look inside and you identify with the peace. When pain is less, there is more time to look outside and identify outward. The mind knows, forgets, then knows again. When this instability is removed, knowledge and peace are established. This is the same process as in samadhi and *vyutthana*.

The mind can switch in a moment from contentment to negativity. What makes us forget to remember divine presence? Distraction and desire will always come, but the aim should not be overtaken. Whenever I go out the door, or start any work, I never forget to remember God. It becomes a habit, but without devotion it is useless.

God's presence is always there. It doesn't come from anywhere outside, but we cannot see it because the passion of rajas and the ignorance of *tamas* veil it. The mind always takes an object. When the body is in pain, pain becomes that object. If your aim is to keep divine presence, then pain as the object of the mind is replaced by constant inner prayer (mantra). This is the keeping of divine presence. Anyone in any condition of life can do Japa Yoga. It works.

You are doing very well in acceptance. In older people negativity develops because the senses cannot cooperate with the desires. So we have to surrender our desires. Now that you have accepted the samskara and are trying to be in peace, nothing more is needed.

Dear I—,

True understanding of death comes through dispassion. Dispassion is developed by regular sadhana.

It's easy to understand the death of a body as the failure of a mechanism. But behind that death of the body there is another death, which is the fear of losing attachment to that body. We have to understand that attachment.

Another death is the death of the ego. A person who does not identify himself as a doer functions in the world like a shadow in a mirror. This person also dies, but their death is to the world and to ignorance. They are immortal. Their fear is totally wiped out.

So the answer of how to get rid of the fear of death is to surrender to God. There is no particular sadhana for overcoming fear of death. When the consciousness rises to higher levels, the pull of attachment loosens.

Dear D—

Death is a reality. No one can avoid it. But it is the fear of death that makes it a horrible thing; otherwise it is a state in which the mind feels intoxicated. There is no fear at the time of death if you accept it as a part of life.

Intellectual understanding of life and death helps in reducing the fear, but real understanding appears in the heart when a person knows that he or she is not the body that dies.

Dear B—,

We inherit the fear of death from past births. Because of this fear the mind dwells on the dark side of life, which are accidents, fires, earthquakes, floods, and sicknesses. All these things are causes of death. These negative thoughts get projected by the mind more toward someone who is close to us than to a person we don't know.

But these negative thoughts are not harmful to others because they arise not from anger but from fear. An example is a mother who can't relax because she always worries that her child may get sick or have an accident. Her mind always focuses on her child. But such thoughts don't cause an accident to happen to her child.

Death is the complement of birth. Together the two are called life. If we don't accept both, we don't accept life. The result is pain, fear, and depression. We know life and death are as inevitable as the rising and setting of the sun. The movement of the sun can't be stopped and neither can birth and death be stopped. One who takes birth will die. It's for sure. Even if one is afraid to die, he or she will still die. This person will live in pain and fear for their whole life, and will die in pain and fear.

If we know that death is an unavoidable thing, then why be afraid? Why make it such a big thing? Death can be an offering to God. God gave us birth and now we are offering this body back to God.

If you understand reality and change your attitude toward death, then there will be no fear, no negativity, and no sadness.

Dear H—,

May God bless you.

The eternal, infinite, all-pervading soul always shines in its own glory. Only the body dies; its reality is created by attachment to the world. Those who are unattached to the world leave the body just as one leaves a worn-out garment.

Keep God's presence in your heart and visualize the light of the soul like a rising sun. Merge in that light and let the flower fall.

Glossary

ahimsa – nonviolence

ajña chakra – the energy center located four fingers in and back from the forehead; the sixth chakra in the shape of a two petal lotus; the seat of concentration

arati – a devotional practice of worshiping with light

asana – yogic posture that purifies the body and mind

ashram – home; spiritual home or center; yogic monastery

ashta sattvik vikara – the eight pure emotions

Ashtanga Yoga – the Yoga of Eight Limbs, an ancient system of yoga including restraints, observances, postures, yogic breathing, withdrawal of the mind from the senses, concentration, meditation, and super-consciousness

atman – the Self, the pure consciousness within the body

avidya – ignorance; the false thought, "I am this mind-body complex;" the association of spirit and matter

bandhas – the three locks (methods of pranayama)

Bhagavad Gita – an ancient text of yoga and Hinudism contained within the epic, *Mahabharata*; the spiritual dialog between Krishna and Arjuna

bija – seed, the essential sound or energetic core of a mantra

Brahman – a name for God; the infinite, formless consciousness; the one without a second

deva – God with a particular name and form; one of the levels of gods *dhyana* – meditation; unbroken concentration on one object

gopis – cowherd girls; female devotees of young Krishna

guru – teacher, spiritual guide

Hatha Yoga – the Yoga of Physical Purification, which emphasizes asanas (postures) and pranayama (yogic breathing) techniques

ishta deva – a devotee's chosen form of God for worship

Ishvara – God with form; the Creator; the union of spirit and matter

Jai Sita Ram – a spiritual greeting that honors the creation; jai = victory, Sita = the earth, the mother, Ram = consciousness, the father; Sita and Ram are the principle characters of the Indian epic, *Ramayana*

japa – repetition (of a mantra) to focus the mind

jiva – the individual; individualized consciousness; consciousness within the subtle body

jñana – knowledge, intellect

Jñana Yoga – the Yoga of Knowledge, which uses intellectual inquiry to transcend the mind

kaivalya – liberation; transcendence of the binding effects of worldly experience; the culmination of samsara

karma – action; the law of cause and effect; the effects on the mind of all past actions

Karma Yoga – the Yoga of Action or Selfless Service, in which the aspirant keeps busy in serving others

kirtan – devotional singing and chanting

Krishna – a famous incarnation of Lord Vishnu, the great preserver; an avatar well known for his playfulness and pranks, whose teachings are recorded in the *Bhagavad Gita*

kundalini – the spiritual energy coiled at the base of the spine that brings enlightenment when awakened

mantra – a spiritual sound, phrase, or prayer

maya – illusion; the creative power of Brahman; literally, "it is and it is not"

mula prakriti – pure matter principle; the root source of all creation

nada – inner sound; the unstruck sound that is heard within

Nada Yoga – the Yoga of Sound, which uses inner sound as the object of concentration

nir-dvandva-avastha – beyond all desires and all attachments to mind, body, and society

Om – the primordial sound of creation; the origin of all sound; signifies the omniscient, omnipresent, omnipotent reality

paramatman – the supreme Self; pure, undifferentiated consciousness

pranayama – yogic breathing exercises, designed to calm the mind; control of life force in the body

puja – devotional worship ceremony

purusha – individual; individualized consciousness; pure undivided consciousness (in its universal aspect) *rajas guna* – quality of activity; restlessness

Ram – a famous incarnation of Lord Vishnu; lead character of the *Ramayana*; known for his adherence to right-eousness; symbol of consciousness or spirit

Ram puja – puja (worship ceremony) performed with Ram as the object of worship

Ramayana – an ancient epic of India telling of the life of Ram, depicting the classic battle of good and evil

sadhana – spiritual practice

sadhu – a wandering practitioner of yoga

samadhi – super-consciousness; the highest stages of meditation; the complete removal of the mind from the world

samsara – the worldly cycle of birth, growth, decay, and death; the wheel of birth, death, and rebirth

samskaras – tendencies; impressions of past actions that become the cause of present and future actions

samyama – a special kind of meditation in which dharana (concentration), dhyana (meditation), and samadhi (super-consciousness) are practiced together

sat – truth; reality; existence; pure

sat guru – the Self; the highest teacher

satsang – the company of truth; spiritual community; a gathering of spiritual people

sattva guna – quality of purity; clarity; light

shaktipat – the transfer of spiritual energy; the process of enlightening a student by the touch of the guru *shanti* – peace

siddha – perfected one; a high saint

siddhi – supernatural power

Sita – wife of Ram; known for her devotion, dedication, and purity; symbol of matter or the earth

sushumna – the subtle nerve channel that flows inside the spinal column and carries kundalini

swami – spiritual preceptor; term of respect; revered

tamas (*guna*) – the quality of inertia; darkness; laziness

tantra – yogic practices that use the senses to go beyond the senses

tapas – austerity or discipline with a spiritual aim

van prastha – forest dweller stage of life; renunciation of worldly pursuits to practice yoga

vyutthana – outward tendency of the mind; worldliness

yoga – union; higher consciousness; the practices of liberation

yogi – one who practices yoga

Sri Rama Foundation was founded to publish the writings of Baba Hari Dass and to support Shri Ram Ashram, an orphanage, school, and free medical clinic near Haridwar, India in the Himalayan foothills. Established by Baba Hari Dass in 1984, the Ashram, shown above, is now home to nearly 50 children. The school, Shri Ram Vidya Mandir, educates over 200 children from kindergarten through ninth grade. A separate facility for the free medical clinic has recently been completed. Please write us at Post Office Box 2550, Santa Cruz, CA 95063 for more information.

Baba Hari Dass has also been the inspiration for several other projects and communities around the world, including the Salt Spring Centre near Vancouver, B.C. The largest project is the Mount Madonna Center in Watsonville, CA. Located on 350 mountain-top acres, the Center offers retreats, workshops, and work-study programs. The Mount Madonna School, located on the same property, is a private pre-kindergarten through 12th grade college preparatory school. For more information, please call 408-847-0406.